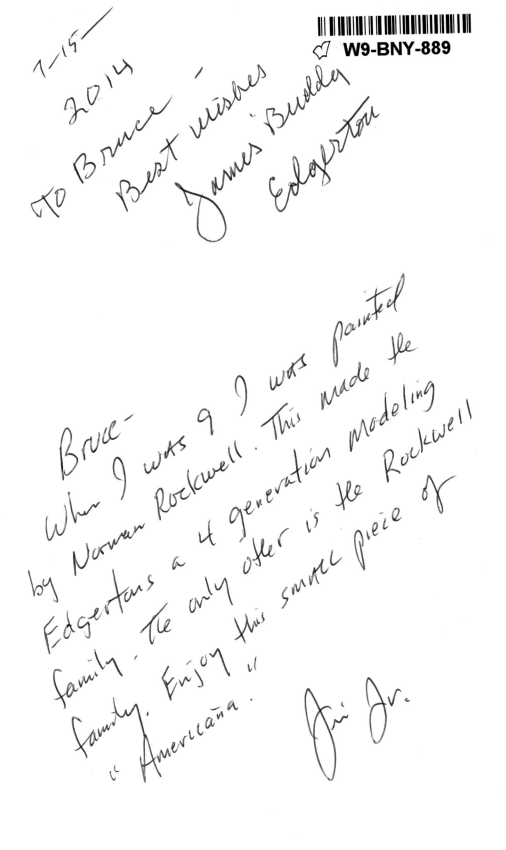

7-15—
2014

(To Bruce —
Best wishes

James Buddy
Edgerton

Bruce—
When I was 9 I was painted
by Norman Rockwell. This made the
Edgertons a 4 generation modeling
family. The only other is the Rockwell
family. Enjoy this small piece of
"Americana."

Jim Jr.

THE UNKNOWN
ROCKWELL

A Portrait of Two American Families

THE UNKNOWN
ROCKWELL

A Portrait of Two American Families

BY JAMES A. "BUDDY" EDGERTON
& NAN O'BRIEN

Foreword by Dick Clark
Television Producer and Media Legend

BATTENKILL RIVER
press

P.O. Box 238, Essex Junction, Vermont 05453
Phone: (802) 778-0305 Fax: (866) 828-4751
www.BattenkillRiverPress.com

Battenkill River Press hardcover 1st edition / October 2009
Printing by King Printing, Lowell, MA

Visit our website at
www.TheUnknownRockwell.com

For more information or special discounts for bulk purchases,
please contact Battenkill River Press at (802) 778-0305 or write to Sales@BattenkillRiverPress.com.

The authors are available for live events. For more information on how to book the authors,
please visit www.TheUnknownRockwell.com, contact us at (802) 778-0305
or email Events@TheUnknownRockwell.com.

Library of Congress Cataloging-in-Publication Data is available

ISBN: 978-0-9677413-6-9

Library of Congress Control Number: 2009906329

Printed in the United States of America
2 4 6 8 9 7 5 3 1

ILLUSTRATION REFERENCE LIST

DEDICATION

To the fond memories of my father and mother, Jim and Clara, and my special friends, Norman and Mary Rockwell; but most of all, to my beautiful wife Dot, who has made continuous sacrifices for me and our family during our wonderful fifty-five years of marriage.

-James A. "Buddy" Edgerton

To my daughters, Elizabeth and Emily, who embraced the decision to move to Vermont so that Buddy's story could be written; to my grown sons, Anthony and Philip, who have always believed in me; and to my husband, Tom, whose love and devotion make all things possible.

-Nan O'Brien

ACKNOWLEDGMENTS

The authors are very grateful to the many people who contributed to the completion of this book and would like to acknowledge their appreciation to the following:

Our most sincere thanks go to Jarvis "Jerry" Rockwell, Thomas "Tommy" Rockwell, and Peter Rockwell for their personal time and their gracious support of this project. The friendship that began more than six decades ago between the Rockwell brothers and Buddy Edgerton continues to be a precious gift.

To the Rockwell Family Agency, our thanks for its licensing assistance and facilitation of the use of the Rockwell illustration images contained within the book.

Thanks to the Norman Rockwell Museum for providing the modeling and illustration images and for being a valuable and rich resource, as well as hosting the launch of The Unknown Rockwell: A Portrait of Two American Families on October 8, 2009. Special thanks to Laurie Norton Moffatt, Director; Rob Doane, Associate Registrar; and Linda Pero, former Curator of the Norman Rockwell Museum.

Edgerton family members who were instrumental in the creation of this book, for which the authors express their thanks, include

Deborah Joy Edgerton; Edith Edgerton Zindle; Joy Edgerton Friezatz; Ardis Edgerton Clark; and Bob and Amy Stroffoleno. Special thanks to Jo and Dave Berry for providing the unknown Rockwell portrait, "Jon."

The authors also wish to thank the following individuals for their time, assistance, and support: Mary Becktoft; Robert Berridge; Martin Oakland; Lynn Swan; Don Trachte; and Cathy Young, Dee Suris, and family.

For providing accommodations during our visits to West Arlington and for allowing us access to the former Rockwell home, we would like to thank the Inn on Covered Bridge Green and its proprietors, Clint and Julia Dickens. We would also like to thank Anne and Ron Weber, for providing us with accommodations. And thanks to Tom Williams, the current owner of the former Edgerton homestead, who welcomed us into his home and gave us the opportunity to reflect and recall memories of long ago.

The authors wish to extend their thanks to Mike McVay and Daniel Anstandig of McVay Media for their media counsel, support, and friendship.

To our counsel and friend, Frank K. Wheaton, Esq., we would like to express our appreciation and thanks for his unwavering patience and commitment, in addition to his extensive legal expertise.

Special thanks to James "Jim" Edgerton, Jr., for his efforts and willingness to do whatever it took to see this project to completion.

To our publisher Tom Bernheim at Battenkill River Press, our deepest gratitude for believing in this project, and for his tireless and conscientious commitment to ensure this historic book had the opportunity to be shared with the public.

FOREWORD

Like millions of Americans, I grew up loving the works of Norman Rockwell. He captured the simple and ordinary in our American way of life. In his paintings, he was able to touch us all with some sort of emotion. When one looks at a collection of his remarkable pictures, it becomes not only a visual experience, but also one with deep feeling.

Like Norman Rockwell himself, James "Buddy" Edgerton paints a portrait with words of New England from the '40s to the '60s. He shares some wonderful stories behind the faces and places in many of Rockwell's paintings. What started as a $5.00 fee for a few hours work turned into a lifetime of memories with Norman Rockwell and his family. Buddy's life was literally a Norman Rockwell painting.

The Unknown Rockwell: A Portrait of Two American Families will create for you a wonderful warm feeling. It's intimate and loaded with moments we can all treasure.

- **Dick Clark**
Television Producer

My very very best
to
my good
friends
Bud
and
Dot
sincerely
Norman
Rockwell

CHAPTER ONE
SOUTH BURLINGTON, VERMONT
2009

My name is James A. Edgerton, Sr., but I have always gone by the name Buddy because my dad was a James, too. I'm seventy-nine years old; I have brown eyes; have shrunk an inch since my youth and now stand at 6'2"; and am on the slim side after years of hard work, a healthy metabolism, a pacemaker that was put in 2001, and triple bypass surgery in early 2005. I still have most of my hair, all of my teeth, and I need glasses to see where I'm going. I've been married for more than fifty-five years to a wonderful woman, Dot, who loves me, supports me, and worries about me when I push myself too hard physically, which - being an honest person - I must confess is more often than it should be for a guy my age.

We live in a modest split-level home in South Burlington, Vermont, a hundred miles from my childhood birthplace of West Arlington, a small farming community of about 2,500 people that lies between the Taconic Range and the Green Mountains, along the Battenkill River. I have two grown children, Jim, Jr., and Deborah Joy, four grandchildren, and a great-granddaughter, who I am proud to say is not only beautiful, but has a cleft in her chin just like her great-grandpa. Jim lives nearby; Deb, whose friends call her Joy, moved back to Vermont from Phoenix two years ago, which has been wonderful for us all.

For more than forty years I have thought about writing my memoirs, and for more than forty years, I have procrastinated, overwhelmed by the thought of having my life on paper for others to see, as - all things being equal - we Vermonters are inclined to be private folks. I wasn't sure it was right to tell what I know. I didn't want to do the wrong thing, so I didn't do it at all. That was the safe choice, and I'm inclined to be conservative in how I approach most things. I also wasn't sure how to even begin writing all of the memories in my head. I could talk for hours and hours, but to sort through and try to make any sense of it for others to read seemed to be a mountain I seriously doubted I could climb.

Well, times change, and old dogs really can learn new tricks, if they're motivated enough, even if I don't actually feel like an old dog yet. In short, I reversed my self-imposed decision to keep quiet and decided that I'd take a stab at it, and if nothing else, it would be a record of our family for future generations. I can't promise you it will be perfect, but I can promise I will do my best to honor the truth as I remember it, which is about all I can do, I suppose. At my age, I'm still pretty good with details, so there'll be plenty of those, but I'm not a flowery-language kind of guy, so don't expect it to be *War and Peace*. My life growing up was simple, and that's what my memoirs will be, too.

To begin with, I was born on March 5, 1930. I'm told my birth took place on a table in the living room of my family's 1812 colonial farmhouse that still sits on River Road, just across the covered bridge from Route 313. The house had been in our family ever since Grandma Buck, my dad's mom, was just six months old. It sat on 212 acres of land, where my dad raised dairy cattle along with chickens, garden produce, and even some potatoes. We had timberland, too. Our farm was self-sufficient, and we felt fortunate to live on a farm during the Depression. Even though we may not have had much in the way of clothes or the nicer things in our home, unlike many people in those times, we always had plenty of food. We marketed milk and eggs, and in the spring when the sap ran, we produced and sold our own maple syrup under the label "Covered Bridge Farm" for obvious reasons. I'll tell you more about all of that later on.

I was the second child of Jim and Clara Edgerton, my sister Edith had arrived a year before me and my sisters Joy, and then Ardis, and my brother, Harold were born in the following six years. Life was not easy for my young parents as they struggled to raise four kids during the Depression, but my mom and dad never complained, they just went about their work with a determined hand and an unswerving belief in the proverbial golden rule, and they instilled that same belief in my sisters and me. We were raised to treat others with respect. We were raised to believe that hard work brought just rewards. We were raised to believe that your word was your bond and that a handshake sealed the deal as well as any piece of paper could. We were raised to believe that doing the right thing was more important than winning. And we were raised not to put on airs or try to be something other than the farm kids that we were. Though mom and dad worked hard, we had what now is called "quality family time," too, with clam bakes and Grange Hall dances and afternoons spent at the local swimming hole on a hot summer's day. Our life was like a Norman Rockwell illustration – because for more than fourteen years Norman Rockwell illustrated our life.

West Arlington (1939) – Our covered bridge, which was build in 1852.

CHAPTER TWO
WEST ARLINGTON, VERMONT
1935 - 1939

1935

In the winter of 1935, my father was twenty-eight years old and my mother was twenty-one. They had been married for six years and already had four children. Life during the Depression was brutal, but it was all we knew. Extended family often lived together under one roof during those times, and our family was no exception. In addition to my parents, three sisters, and me, the Edgerton household included my dad's parents; my grandfather's younger brother, Uncle Charlie; and my dad's fourteen-year old sister, Amy. My sisters shared a bedroom; Amy had her own bedroom, as did my parents and grandparents; Uncle Charlie slept in the "summer rooms" of our house, a sort of unheated annex with three bedrooms, a parlor, a kitchen and a pantry that my grandparents typically lived in during the summer months; and I slept on a daybed that had been set-up in the crook of the upstairs landing. A crib always stood in my parents' room.

We did not have electricity in our house; we used kerosene lamps, carrying them from room-to-room as need be, except for one fancy kerosene lamp that always sat in the middle of the table in the far corner of our downstairs parlor. I can still see my mother holding a lamp high above her head to give us kids light as we climbed the stairs to go to bed, our flickering shadows from the glowing lamp playing against the staircase and up the walls, into the darkness. In the barn, kerosene lanterns crusted with manure hung on the walls to provide light for the men to hand-milk the cows and do other morning chores before the sun came up, and finish the evening chores after the sun had gone down.

Our house had three wood stoves, one in the kitchen, one in the living room, and one in the parlor. A huge woodshed out back held about eight to ten cords of wood - more than a thousand cubic feet - that my dad had cut, which lasted us through the winter months. The kitchen stove had a hot water reservoir, an oven, and surface area for cooking. A big, black heavy flatiron always sat on it, too. I still can't figure out how my mother made such wonderful pies in a wood-burning stove, but I suppose cooking daily for ten people gave her lots of practice.

The three stoves were our only sources of heat during the long, hard Vermont winters. Between the three, the downstairs was easily warmed. Upstairs, there were three or four air ducts in the floors that allowed some of the stoves' heat to reach the bedrooms, but around midnight or one o'clock in the morning the fires would die down, and that pretty much was the end of the heat while we slept. There were times it was so cold that by the time we woke up, the floorboards upstairs were frozen. As soon as she got up every morning, my mother would start up the stoves again, the first of her many morning tasks. When my sisters and I woke up, we would bring our clothes downstairs and get dressed in the warmth of the parlor stove, racing to see who could get dressed the fastest, motivated by the cold.

The winter of 1935, I started helping my mom with my very first farm chore. I had to fetch and carry the wood from the shed and fill the wood boxes that stood by each stove. They had to be kept full at all times, which meant they had to be replenished daily, a big responsibility. I was not quite five years old.

Without electricity, we didn't have indoor plumbing either, not even a bathroom, since there was no power mechanism to route the water in or out of the house. The path to the outdoor privy was quite "well-worn," you might say. In the nighttime, everyone had a night pot beneath the bed so that you didn't have to go outside if you couldn't wait to go till morning. You could buy night pots that were pretty fancy, painted or with lids on them, but ours were just tin pots that did the job. The first chore my six-year old sister, Edith, had each morning was to empty the pots; I was really glad she was the oldest of the Edgerton kids.

On Saturday nights we all had our weekly bath and got our hair washed, too. We bathed in a big metal washtub that was set up in the kitchen where it was warm. With no running water in the house - "running water" to us meant running with the bail pail in your hand! - one of the adults had to carry water in from the well, then it would be heated up on the stove and, finally, poured into the washtub. Most of the time, we all used the same bath water because it took a lot of work to fill the tub even once. We washed in order of age, oldest to youngest, so my sister Ardis always had the last bath. Winter baths took up the whole Saturday evening; it was much easier in the summer months when you could grab your soap and stand out in the rain or run down to the swimming hole to get clean.

Laundry was a huge chore for the women in our house. With dirty clothes from ten people (who only took a bath once a week) and bed linens that had to be washed weekly, doing laundry took an entire day. Fortunately (or, I suspect, because my mother put her foot down) one of the few modern items we had in our house was a gasoline-powered washing machine. It was a slick invention, the gas-powered machine, a combination washtub and gas engine that was all housed in a metal stand. The washtub sat on the top of the stand and the engine sat openly directly below it on a small shelf. The warning on the side of the engine cautioned you not to let the clothes come in contact with the hot exhaust hose or engine, and you had to make sure to open the door to let the exhaust fumes out.

The whole contraption was on wheels so it could be moved into the kitchen when it was being used. Mom heated up the water on the stove in a big iron pot and then carefully poured the water into the tub. After adding laundry soap and a small amount of clothes, she would fire up the engine and it would automatically agitate the clothes, saving my mom from having to scrub them against a washboard. I can still hear the sound of the engine as it chug-chug-chugged along, whipping the clothes around the basin and beating the farm dirt (and worse) out of all of our clothes. When the agitating was done, my mom would take the clothes out and pile them on the kitchen table, empty the dirty soapy water, and put more hot, clean water and clothes back in the tub, then fire up the engine again. When the second cycle was done, she would run the clothes through the ringers that sat on the side of the washer to squeeze out the water and then take the clothes outside to hang on a clothesline to dry, no matter how cold it was. Sometimes when Mom brought the clothes back inside during the winter, the clothes were frozen stiff from the cold and she had to put them near the parlor woodstove to soften up before ironing them with the black flatiron. It would have made some sort of sense, I suppose, to have hung the clothes inside, but the only room that she might have been able to do that was the cellar, and that was already filled with potatoes, onions, carrots, and other food that we stored to eat during the winter. Plus, Mom would never have standed for our clothes to smell like onions.

In any small farm community, everyone pretty much knows everything about everyone else, and West Arlington was no different. It's not that folks were nosy, it's just that you couldn't help noticing when, say, a guy and a girl were sweet on one another, or a young couple had a baby on the way, or someone took sick. But more importantly, our phone system also kept everyone in the know, even if it wasn't designed that way. There were no private phone lines in West Arlington, we only had a party line. Those of you as old as I am know what I'm talking about, but those of you who are younger probably are a bit lost right now, so let me explain.

Everyone had a physical phone in their own house, but there was only one phone line – just one line that everyone in the West Arlington Valley had to share, and that's why it was called a "party line." Each household had a position on the party line that was designated by a certain number of rings. Our house was fifth, and so our signal was five short rings – ring-ring-ring-ring-ring! The houses that were after ours on the party line had a different signal, kind of like Morse Code, with dots and dashes. The folks who were sixth had one long ring – riiiinnnng! – followed by one short ring – ring! Number seven on the party line had one long ring followed by two short rings, number ten was two long rings, and so on, the number of rings increasing each time folks decided to get service. Whenever the phone rang, we all stopped what we were doing like playing a game of statues, and counted to see if the call was for us.

The system worked in most ways, but it did have its drawbacks. First of all, everyone knew who was getting a call because we knew one another's ring patterns. Secondly, if someone were using the party line, it was unavailable to everyone else. Third, anyone and everyone could listen in on the line when a call came through to you. To be fair, sometimes you accidentally miscounted the number of rings and picked up when the call wasn't for you. But more often than not, a "click" on the line let you know that someone else had been listening in or had tried to discreetly hang up after getting an earful. It wasn't polite to eavesdrop, but it wasn't uncommon, either. Even my Grandma Wilcox would listen in sometimes. One time I watched as she reached up and grabbed a hold of the pendulum in her big grandfather's clock and held it so no one would hear she was listening on the line. When she hung up, she let go of the pendulum and then reached in her big pocketbook, took out a nickel, and reaching down to me, she wrapped it in my handkerchief before patting me on the head with a wink and shooing me out the door.

That winter, I was still way too young to help my dad with the heavy chores, but during the Depression it was not unusual for men to come by our farm offering to work for a meal, or perhaps even just a bit of food, before going on their way. If my dad had work that someone could do, he was glad to exchange the labor for food; we had plenty of food on the farm, but not much cash, so it was a win-win. Sometimes the men stayed a day; sometimes they even lived with us for a bit, depending on the season and what had to be done. It never occurred to us that there was any threat to having what amounted to drifters in our home, my parents treated each person who wanted to work with respect, and we never had any problems.

The day seventeen-year old Bob Stroffoleno strode up to our house was pretty much like every other wintry day in West Arlington. Snow was on the ground, the temperature was hovering near zero, the wind swirled down off the mountain behind our house, wailing through the line of maple trees out back. Like many others, Bob had come to the house looking for work. He was a handsome guy with a warm smile, and I remember my dad was impressed that he appeared strong, enthusiastic, and – most importantly - willing to work long hours in exchange for room, board, laundry, and a mere five dollars per month. On a handshake, Bob was hired, and the two quickly developed a brotherly friendship in addition to their work alliance. Bob didn't even mind when, on more than a few occasions, my dad "borrowed" the five dollars he gave him in wages from the top drawer of Bob's dresser, and then gave it back to him when the milk check came in.

February 1st

Uncle Charlie was a big man who had worked hard all of his life. As a kid, I didn't know much about him other than he was a lifelong bachelor and had lived with us as long as I could remember; he was a fun, older guy with a quick smile and a big laugh who helped with the farm chores whenever he could; and he loved my mother's pies. He played with us kids, too, and would wink at you when he secretly gave you a penny. Everyone should have an Uncle Charlie.

One morning I was sitting alone at the kitchen table eating my breakfast, slowly pushing my eggs around the plate. My younger sisters had already finished eating and I could hear them playing in the parlor, Edith had left for school. I had been the last at the table to finish because I had been the last to get up. Some days it was just too cold to want to come out from under the pile of warm covers. My mom stood over near the woodstove preparing the second round of breakfast for the men when all of a sudden our attention was caught by the sound of my father coming in from the barn, his footsteps sounding slower and heavier than usual. Both my mom and I looked up to see my father, carrying Uncle Charlie on his back. My dad met my mom's gaze and he slowly shook his head, his eyes a little watery, but not much. Her eyes filled up, too, as she turned back to the stove and tended to her cooking and he took Uncle Charlie into the small bedroom beside the parlor. Neither said a word.

The next day, Dad put up the funeral wreath on the door to let folks know we'd had a death in the family. Uncle Charlie had lived to see seventy Vermont winters. When he passed, he left my father his entire estate - $139 and change, out of which my dad had to pay an $8 court fee. It was a real windfall; but we all would rather have had our Uncle Charlie.

1936

February

West Arlington is a rural area that sits just a few miles west of a slightly bigger town, Arlington. There's an East Arlington, too, right where you'd expect it to be. The whole general area is known as "Arlington," but for Vermonters who live in the area, there is a difference.

Our house in West Arlington was on River Road, an unpaved country road that ran east and west, parallel to both the Battenkill River and Vermont State Route 313. Route 313 and Route 7A intersect in Arlington. To reach our house from Arlington, you headed west from 7A onto 313 and traveled about 4.2 miles, then took another left across the covered bridge that spanned the Battenkill and onto a dirt road that didn't have a name when I was growing up, but is called "Covered Bridge Road" now. Once you crossed the covered bridge, our house sat a few hundred yards directly in front of you on the left, next door to the old abandoned Otis property on the right. The land from the covered bridge to our house was a large, open grassy area known as "the Green." On the right side of the Green there was a white, painted church with a pavilion behind it that housed our Grange dances in the summertime; the Church Annex, which we used in the Grange Hall, was next door to the church; and on the left side of the Green was our one-room schoolhouse.

My dad owned the land that the schoolhouse sat on, but he never charged the school board for using it. After my mom lit the wood stoves in our house each morning, she'd walk down to the schoolhouse and light the wood stove there, too. By the time the students arrived a few hours later, the school was toasty warm. Since there was no running water at the schoolhouse, the drinking water for the students was a bucket with a ladle that everyone shared, hung on a nail in the back of the room. My mom filled the bucket from our well each morning, too, then headed back up the dirt drive to get the rest of her morning chores done before the sun came up and the men came in from milking the cows, hungry for breakfast. It wasn't easy for my mom that winter, trudging in the pre-dawn hours up and down the unpaved drive in freezing temperatures; she was heavily pregnant with her fifth child.

February was a particularly cold and snowy month, and on the 20th, the temperatures hit more than twenty below zero. Bob still lived with us, had been with us for more than a year, and in that time he had become like a member of the family. He came into the house from milking the cows, bundled in long underwear and woolen shirts layered under heavy sweaters and a stout winter coat, his head covered with a fur-lined cap. He was reaching down to get his work boots off. Suddenly, he saw something down toward the covered bridge. Standing up and crossing to the front window for a second look, Bob was horrified to see smoke spiraling up in the air from inside the schoolhouse. He raced into the front hall closet, grabbed our fire extinguisher, a small handheld contraption that used a chemical liquid loaded in a canister, and bolted out the front door past my dad who was just coming in.

"The schoolhouse is on fire!" Bob screamed, and with that, my dad turned and grabbed a small throw rug from the hallway as he, too, ran out the door, flying down the snow-covered dirt road behind Bob toward the school.

Bob and my dad battled the blaze alone that freezing cold February morning. There was no fire department to be summoned, no 911 call to be made, no running water to pump onto the flames, and no other men close by to help. Bob aimed the fire extinguisher at the bigger areas, as my dad beat back the smaller flames with the rug, in a kind of well-choreographed dance borne of both desperation and mutual trust. It looked like they were going to get it put out, when all of a sudden the fire extinguisher pressure dropped and the chemical spray that had been pouring out of the nozzle suddenly began spurting, gurgling, and then, finally, dripping to nothingness. The chemical liquid had run out.

Without any way to control the larger flames, my dad and Bob stood back and watched helplessly as the fire roared back up and engulfed the school, burning the structure to the ground which was, thankfully, covered with snow, keeping the fire from spreading any further. By then, my mother, grandparents, Aunt Amy, and my sisters and I had put on our hats and coats and gloves, and had slowly walked to where Bob and my dad were standing.

"One more gallon of chemical in the pump and I coulda put it out," said Bob sadly, shaking his head.

Thursday, March 5th

I woke up excited for two reasons on this day. One, it was my sixth birthday, and that meant a few presents and a special birthday cake, with singing and blowing out candles and wishes made. Two, today was the day that the fall first-graders-to-be got to visit the school and meet the teacher and the other kids, and talk about what it was going to be like in first grade. At the thought of going to school, I was excited and scared all at the same time.

Since the fire had destroyed the schoolhouse, classes were temporarily being held in the Grange Hall. Mid-morning, my mom took me by the hand and led me down the road and walked up the steps to the Grange Hall door. Without knocking, she quietly opened the door and slipped in, leading me to the side of the room where a few other kids and their moms stood, to wait for Miss Pye to tell us what to do. We didn't have to wait long. Just a few minutes after my mom and I walked in, the nineteen-year old teacher clapped her hands with delight and turned to us.

"Welcome!" she said, smiling a warm smile. "Let's go down the row, and tell me your name and something special about yourself."

One by one, the other kids stepped forward and said their name and told something unique – "I have a dog," "I like to draw," "I'm good at throwing a ball," and so on until it was my turn. Suddenly, my mouth went dry and I wasn't sure what to say or do. Miss Pye stood there, quietly waiting, as I pulled back and partially hid from her gaze behind my mother's very pregnant belly, saying nothing.

"Buddy! Go ahead!" my sister Edith loudly whispered from the second graders' row.

"My name is Buddy Edgerton, and…and…"

"And what, Buddy?" asked the pretty, young, Miss Pye sweetly and oh, so patiently. "Can you think of something special about you to tell me?"

I felt myself start to blush when, all of a sudden, it hit me.

"and - TODAY IS MY BIRTHDAY!" I proclaimed loudly.

"Whooo-hooo!" All of the kids yelled and clapped, and some of the bigger boys came over and gave me a pretend spanking – "One! Two! Three! Four! Five! Six! – And one for good luck!" they said, cheering. It was a glorious day.

Thursday, March 12th

The lumber for the new school had been delivered and sat waiting on the Green. The charred remains of the old schoolhouse had been cleared away and construction on the new school was going to start soon. A local architect had already been hired to design a new, *modern* one room schoolhouse, and Cliff Wilcox had been hired as the contractor on the job. He had promised the school board that the new school would be ready in time for September, my first day in first grade.

The week after my birthday it was much warmer and we had rain occasionally mixed with a little snow almost everyday. At times, it rained heavily. The warm moisture melted the foot of snow that had been on the ground, gradually saturating the earth and turning everything to mud and slush. Still the rain came. The Battenkill River was rising and rising and when it reached the bottom of the covered bridge, and spilled up and over its banks and even then it kept on rising, toward the pile of lumber that was going to be our school. We watched out the parlor window helplessly, as big sheets of rain battered the windows and small, swift running currents poured down the back pasture, creating make-shift ditches between our house and the old Otis property before running down across the Green. And still it rained, the sky was one endless gray cloud that never moved, never brightened, never let up.

Seventy miles to the east, the flood waters lifted the Central Vermont Railroad Bridge up from its stone footings and washed it into the river. The ironwork spans, too heavy to be washed downstream, sank to the river's floor. We had a small old radio with big batteries and we listened as word came from other parts of New England that the water was rising there as well. The dam at New Hartford, Connecticut burst, leaving fourteen thousand people homeless. The Connecticut River crested at an incredible thirty-seven and a half feet. In Massachusetts, ten people died and fifty thousand were left homeless, with more than $200,000,000 damage - in 1936 dollars, not current dollars, mind you. And still the rain came. The water swelled higher and higher onto the Green, almost reaching the lumber, almost sweeping it away, almost destroying our schoolhouse again, before it was even built, before I could even attend my first day of first grade.

Sunday morning, March 22nd, the sun started to shine through the still-gray clouds. The Great Flood of 1936, the worst flood in 20th century New England, had finally come to an end. And as we cautiously peeked out the parlor window one more time, we could see that our school lumber was still sitting in a pile on the Green, miraculously untouched.

Wednesday, April 15th

I don't remember a lot about my brother Harold when he was born, other than I remember that in the middle of his back there was a bump on his spine that looked like a small tomato, open and cut in half. I didn't remember seeing anything that looked like that when my sister Ardis was born, and even though I was only six, I knew something wasn't right. The worried look on my parents' faces also told me something wasn't right. After my sisters and I had finally been allowed to come into my parents' room and peer in at our new baby brother lying in the crib at the foot of their bed, we were quickly whooshed out of the room by my dad, and he closed the door firmly behind us. We knew my mom would need quiet and sleep after giving birth, so Edith picked up Ardis and headed outside, with Joy and me following behind.

It had rained off and on all morning and the grass was still a bit damp. We played One Potato Two Potato, Fox & Geese, Hide 'n' Seek, and finally Tag. I let my two and a half-year old sister, Ardis, "catch" me and she just giggled and giggled. After running around for a while, we all stretched out in the front yard on our backs, gazing up at the cloudy sky, looking for shapes and trying to figure out what to do next.

"Let's go over to the haunted house!" I whispered to Edith, motioning next door.

The Otis property, which had been built in 1792, stood less than twenty yards from our house, to the right if you stood at the covered bridge looking across the Green. Everyone called it the haunted house because in 1916, the owners had skipped town and abandoned it so quickly that they left wood neatly stacked in the shed, canned goods neatly stacked in the pantry, household furniture and items in place, and doors unlocked. We don't exactly know why the owners left, but we felt pretty sure it had to be something scandalous, to leave so abruptly. The barn had gradually caved in over time, so my dad had salvaged the old boards and timber and used it as fuel for the evaporator at our sap house, necessary to produce our famous homemade maple syrup. The crop land had become overgrown, turning to brush filled with small trees growing everywhere. But, the home's foundation had remained solid, the slate roof survived the years well, and the brick smokehouse was in good repair.

"Uh-uh, *you* go if you want," said Edith, shaking her head, "not me!"

"Come with me, Edith!" I said.

"No!" she replied firmly.

"Pleeeeeeezzzzeee?" I said, flashing my biggest grin at her, "please come with me?"

"Why?" said Edith, "Are you afraid to go alone? Are you a scaredy-cat?"

"No!" I protested, glancing away from her eyes.

"Yes you are, you're a scaredy-cat. Scaredy-cat! Scaredy-cat!" she sing-songed.

"I am not!" I said loudly, my voice rising, "I'm going to go over there right now and I think *you're* the scaredy-cat because you won't come with me!"

"No," said Edith, shaking her head matter-of-factly, "I have to watch Ardis, she's too little to run away if any ghosts come out - but I'll watch you to make sure you're safe."

I wasn't too sure I wanted to go alone, but it had become a matter of pride at that point and I didn't want my sister to think I was afraid. I slowly got up, took a big breath, and hesitantly took a few steps.

"Look in the window and see if you can see any ghosts!" said Joy, clapping her hands excitedly.

I stopped in my tracks at that, my eyes wide at the thought, and then turned my head and looked back at the three girls sitting there, waiting for me to cross the invisible line of both our property and my courage. Ardis had climbed up into Edith's lap. She was twisted around and looking up at her, batting at her hair, and Joy was snuggled in next to her.

"Go on, Buddy!" said Edith in a loud whisper, "You can do it!"

Taking a big breath, I turned around and counted to three to myself, then suddenly I sprinted forward toward the Otis' front door and peered in through the small side windows. They were covered with dirt and I used the arm of my jacket to wipe off a small spot so I could look in, but all I could see were different shapes and shadows. I squinted my eyes, trying to adjust to the darkness inside, when suddenly I felt something touching my leg! Letting out a yell, I turned and ran like crazy back to our yard and to the safety of my sisters, crushing the tall weeds that the wind had brushed against my leg only moments before.

Tuesday, September 8, 1936

The new schoolhouse was ready, as promised. At precisely 8:00 a.m., Miss Pye came out the front door and rang the big school bell, signaling all of the students to gather and form an orderly line to enter the classroom. She smiled and waited patiently as the students hurried into place. Edith grabbed my arm and took me to the front of the line.

"This is where *you* stand," she whispered knowingly in my ear, "the first graders are always at the front of the line, you have to stand in order of youngest to oldest. *I* have to stand back there," she said proudly, motioning behind us. I was really glad to have an older, smarter sister with me that first morning.

The inside of the school was - even to a six year old boy - beautiful. An indoor bathroom was in one corner, and a bubble fountain that worked using gravity stood in the other. There was no water pail and ladle hanging from a nail on *these* walls. In the back of the classroom there was even a small kitchenette. A larger and more efficient wood furnace kept the room warm. When the weather turned cold, my mom continued to start up the furnace in the morning before school started, but the wood burned longer and more efficiently throughout the day so that the students and Miss Pye didn't have to work so hard at keeping the fire burning.

I took my seat in the front row and followed Miss Pye's directions, raising my hand when I knew the answer and listening carefully when I didn't. I worked quietly as she taught the second graders their lessons, the third graders theirs, and before I knew it, it was time for lunch. Miss Pye dismissed us and we filed out, single file. This time, I knew to take my place in the front of the line. Once outside, Edith and I raced home to eat our lunch, ducked out back to wave to my dad in the field, and then, when Miss Pye rang the school bell again, returned to our classroom for our afternoon lessons.

Looking back, it's amazing to me to think that a nineteen-year old teacher would have the responsibility of educating thirty students ranging from first through sixth grades, though the majority of them were in the younger grades. Most kids in our town didn't go to school past the eighth grade, the families were so poor that they needed their sons to work and their daughters to help at home. My parents could have made the same choice, but they didn't – in our house, education was valued and doing well was important. The Edgerton kids didn't just show up at school, we worked; we took full advantage of the time away from the farm; we appreciated the opportunity to learn. I knew that school was important if I were going to be somebody, someday, even if that meant simply being the best darn dairy-farming-somebody in all of West Arlington, Vermont.

Friday, December 4th

A few days after Thanksgiving, my parents had taken my baby brother to the hospital in Troy, New York, for an operation. Dr. Harvey, who had repaired two hernias for my dad, thought he might be able to fix the bump on Harold's back, too. Turns out, Harold had been born with Spina Bifida. Despite Doc Harvey's best efforts, Harold passed away on December 4th at the age of seven months. I remember seeing the small casket at the funeral, but not much else.

I will never know how my Dad paid for the surgery and hospital bills. I suspect, though, that Doc Harvey found a way around it so that the financial problem didn't add to the burden of my parents losing their baby boy. Doc was a famous surgeon before he ever met our family, and he had a reputation of being a generous man. I know it broke his heart that he couldn't fix Harold.

Doc kept in close contact with my folks after that, and he and my dad developed a warm friendship. He came to the farm and hunted deer with my dad on many occasions. That Christmas, each of us kids got a big surprise, our very own Flexible Flyer sleds. I later learned Doc had played Santa. Even though he couldn't save our brother, he had wanted to do something special for us.

No one ever talked much about Harold's passing, that's not how we Vermonters are, but Harold's loss left an empty place in my parents' heart and in my parents' room, and my dad finally put the crib away for good.

1936 was one heck of a year.

1937

Spring

The weather had turned warm only a few weeks before, and with it had come the unpredictable weather of a Vermont Spring – blue skies in the mornings, light rain in the afternoons, clear starlit skies at night. The bulbs were pushing up and the air finally smelled more like sunshine than snow. My dad readied the farm equipment for summer haying and fixed the pasture fences if they needed it. The fields had to be "broken up," preparing the ground for Spring planting. We had beans, turnips, rhubarb, and tomatoes. We grew potatoes, beets, carrots, sweet corn, and pumpkins. We had corn for silage for our farm animals, and three or four rows of popping corn for ourselves. There were apple trees on our property, too.

That Spring also brought a lot of strangers to West Arlington. A team of men from the local electric company were canvassing the town, house by house, clipboard and pen in hand, to ask if we would be willing to pay for electrical service. My parents, like everyone else in West Arlington, eagerly voted yes, and after a majority "yea" consensus was reached, plans were begun to hook us up. For the next few months the workers scurried all over town digging holes, setting poles, and climbing like monkeys to string the wires. Orange Baker, an actual Green Mountain Boys descendant and the only electrician in town, was kept busy pulling wires through houses and barns, and installing light fixtures on ceilings and walls in homes up and down the river. We didn't know exactly when the magic switch would be flipped, and after the initial excitement, we kids soon forgot all about it.

North Bennington Bank finally foreclosed on the old Otis property and put it up for auction. My dad bought the land – thirty acres for ten dollars an acre – and the house was sold to two Mount Vernon, New York couples, Art and Effie Deverman, and Stanley and Peggy Griffis. The couples had formed a partnership and were going to create a "tourist home" out of the property. Tourist homes were big in that time, but we never understood why.

Wealthy people from outside New York City would pay money to come all the way to Vermont, put on work clothes, and then labor in the fields for fun. They marveled at how it was to "rough it" in the countryside. The guests weren't steady help, and weren't that good of help either, but they had fun and were ok for city slickers. It was all in the perspective, I suppose. I guess the tourists thought it was quaint to pay to pretend to be Vermont farmers for a few days; we just thought, for folks you'd think would know better, it wasn't real smart.

Effie Deverman and Stanley Griffis were brother and sister. Both the Griffis and the Devermans had family in the Arlington area and had always loved visiting in the summertime, and when they saw the opportunity to purchase the Otis property for a bargain price, they snapped it up. Art took a job at the Mack Molding Company as an accountant while Effie, Stanley, and Peggy tended to the property.

I don't think Peggy was particularly thrilled with that arrangement. I hate to say it, but I never remember her having a kind word for anybody, she said nothing or she was cross. My strongest memory of her is one day when I went over to listen to a Brooklyn Dodger game on their radio. The reception on our little radio wasn't so good, and Art had told me it was ok if I came over to catch a few innings on their console radio. Peggy came into the parlor and, seeing me spread out on the floor, snapped, "Don't you have anything better to do?" I high-tailed it out the door, embarrassed and disappointed, but I never said anything about it to Art. After that, I just sneaked over when I knew she wasn't around.

The Devermans had one son, Stan, named after his uncle.

He was five years older than I was and quickly became like a big brother to me, a welcome relief from having to constantly deal with three sisters. And, Stan was a big help to my dad on the farm in the years before I was old enough to help. He was a strong teenage boy and my dad taught him a lot about working on a farm. He learned quickly and was eager to work alongside my dad, helping with the cattle; chopping wood, sugaring, haying; my dad let him drive our team of horses, Dick and Prince, the ultimate sign of trust from my father. The first time he asked me to play catch, he even let me wear his baseball glove. I almost didn't know what to do. Normally, I just caught the baseball bare-handed, we didn't have enough money for luxuries like baseball gloves. I followed Stan around like a puppy dog and, to his credit, he never chased me off - after more than seventy years, we're still friends to this day.

Saturday, May 8th

My dad put the funeral wreath back up on the door. My grandfather, Albert Edgerton, passed on this day at the age of seventy-eight. It rained off and on all day, sort of like the mood of our house; we alternately laughed about his jokes and were somber about his loss. My grandmother said very little, she just sat in the corner of the parlor and did what respectful folks do when their husbands pass and they suddenly become the matriarch of a family. Her hands were clasped, a handkerchief tightly clutched in her fist, and she dabbed at her eyes once in a while when she thought no one was looking, before wearily excusing herself and climbing the stairs alone for the night.

Mid-December

Our woodlot always had the best Christmas trees in West Arlington. Each year we would traipse through the lot looking for the perfect spruce for our house. My dad would cut it down and skillfully drag it around the other trees without breaking any of its branches, through the snow and into the house, and we would spend a special evening setting it up in the corner of the parlor, decorating it with simple, handmade ornaments, popcorn strings, and candy canes. The scent of fresh cut spruce would fill the room and everyone was happy. Once, my dad even grabbed my mom's hand and swung her - surprised and giggling – around the room, singing Tommy Dorsey's song, "I'm In A Dancing Mood."

"Yuck," I said, making a face.

"You're too young to understand," replied my nine-year old sister, Edith, sighing, looking dreamily at our folks.

That year, I proudly marched to the front of the classroom and informed Miss Pye that my father's Christmas trees were the best in all of the world and that he had said he would donate one of his special trees to the schoolhouse; then, I brazenly informed her that the condition was, it would be necessary for *me* to guide the older boys to the perfect tree, as only I knew where on our woodlot it could be found. She started to say something, then caught herself and, smiling sweetly, gave us permission to head for the woods. It took us two hours away from our lessons, but we found a beaut, and the big boys hauled it down the mountain, across the Green, and into our classroom.

There was an added excitement hanging in the air that day.

It wasn't just the growing anticipation of Santa's arrival, it was palpable, something that even today I can't quite put into words – but we all sensed it, felt it, that something was different and that something big was just around the corner.

Friday, December 17th

My parents seemed to be exchanging secretive glances and smiles more than the pre-Christmas knowing looks that usually passed between them during the holiday time. My mom had fixed an early supper, and my dad had remained at the table for a bit after we were done.

"Grab your coats and let's all go out and see what the weather's doin'," my dad slowly said, my mom trying hard not to smile.

"Do I have to put my boots on?" asked Ardis as she dutifully put on her coat and looked up at him.

"No, sweetie, jump up here," he replied, holding his arms out to her.

Obliging, she ran to him, unbuttoned coat flying, and leapt up trustfully. His powerful arms swooped her up in the air high above his head before gently placing her on his shoulders. And with that, he walked out the door onto the front lawn, with all of us expected to follow.

We quietly stood in the darkness of the front yard, small clouds of breath coming from our mouths as we slowly breathed the freezing cold in and out. Edith, Joy, and I were fidgeting and giggling, not quite sure what we were supposed to be looking at as we stood beside our parents, who were still as statues.

"Mom?" I finally whispered, "what – "

"Buddy - sshh!" said my dad softly.

We stood still another few minutes and my legs started to get cold and cramped from not moving around. My hands were jammed into my pockets because I had forgotten my gloves as we were rushed out the door.

At precisely 6:00 p.m., a sudden burst of light lit up the entire sky over the Valley as electricity surged through the wires and connected with home after home like a wave, rushing toward us at an incredible speed. Literally screaming with delight, we all made a beeline into the house, running from room to room, flipping the long forgotten switches, making the lights go on-off-on-off! Ardis wiggled out of my dad's arms and ran into the parlor, and her eyes flew wide open.

"Look! Look!" she squealed, pointing, as she jumped up and down, her red curls flying.

And there in the corner of the parlor sat the most perfect spruce tree from my father's most perfect Christmas tree lot, sparkling and twinkling with strings and strings of colored lights. Perfect.

1938

Spring

The snow stopped falling and the Spring thaw arrived as it always did, and with it came an exciting renovation at the Edgerton house – one of our bedrooms had been emptied, and my dad and Bob were transforming it into a real live, indoor bathroom! For days they hammered and painted behind the closed door, making loud thumping noises over our heads, but we weren't allowed to go in. Finally, early one evening my dad called everyone upstairs and grandly turned the glass doorknob, opening the door and slowly motioning us inside.

We all let out a collective "Ahhhhh!" as we walked into the room. Next to a sink against the wall stood one of the most wondrous sights Edith had ever seen – a porcelain toilet.

"No more night pot emptying for me!" she announced.

A bathtub sat on four legs, gleaming white, at the far end of the room. We couldn't even imagine the luxury of having hot and cold running water by simply turning a faucet. All of us gathered around as my father demonstrated which was hot, which was cold. He plugged the drain with a little black rubber cork strung on a chain to fill the tub, then showed us how to gently pull on the chain to unplug it so the water could flow out. We watched, fascinated, as the water rushed toward the drain, gravity creating a small tornado of water as it swirled into the pipes for a mysterious unknown destination, a faint sucking noise as it disappeared for good.

"And no more dirty bath water for *me*!" declared Ardis loudly, as we all laughed and danced around the bathroom.

Tuesday, September 6th

The school bell rang loudly through the Valley and all of the kids came running. Coming up behind Edith, I grabbed Joy by the hand and took her to the front of the line.

"This is where *you* stand," I whispered knowingly in her ear, "the first graders are always at the front of the line, you have to stand in order of youngest to oldest. *I* have to stand back there," I said proudly, motioning behind us. I'm sure she was really glad to have an older, smarter brother with her that first morning.

As we all settled into our places in line, I looked up expecting to see Miss Pye and was startled to see an older woman instead. We followed the new teacher into our classroom, where she informed us that her name was Mrs. Fitzgerald and that she was going to be our new teacher. She told us that Miss Pye had gotten married and had moved to Cambridge, New York.

Mrs. Fitzgerald was a matronly woman, a good-sized woman, too. She stood about five foot nine or ten, and could pick up even the bigger kids by the back of the neck when she had to. Her style was different than Miss Pye's, quite the disciplinarian, but she was also a very good teacher. For the times, Mrs. Fitzgerald was very innovative in what she taught us. One day at the beginning of the year she quieted everyone down and addressed everyone in the classroom.

"How many of you have toothbrushes?" she asked.

Out of thirty students, about half raised their hands. A slight look of dismay crossed her face, which she quickly hid.

"Well!" she said, "Starting tomorrow, we will all study dental hygiene *together*."

And true to her word, the next day each child received a dental hygiene lesson - and a brand new toothbrush.

Wednesday, September 21st

Like most farmers, my dad kept a small tabletop radio, a Crosley, in the barn that he turned on as soon as he started morning chores and left on until the chores were done. He turned it on for two reasons: (1) To receive the farm reports from WGY-Schenectady, a 50K-watt station that provided weather and other important farm information to the region; and (2) to serenade the cows. Farmers always believed that cows gave more milk when music was on, simple as that! Our cows seemed to particularly like country music.

For four days New England was pummeled with rain, and folks were worried, remembering all too well the Great Flood of 1936. The weatherman also mentioned a hurricane out in the Atlantic, which had turned and was heading north. Over the next few days, we heard more reports about the path of the hurricane. By the time it was off the coast of the Carolinas it had weakened, but it had also picked up speed.

At exactly 9:00 p.m. on September 21st, what would later be called the Great New England Hurricane made landfall, hitting Connecticut the hardest as it came on shore. Unfortunately, the hurricane struck during the peak of high tide, adding to the destruction. Because of its strength and speed, the hurricane didn't even weaken as it made landfall, and as it turned north, its eye went directly over West Arlington. By the time the hurricane was over, more than seven hundred people were dead and more than two thousand were injured, with damage estimated at more than $400 million in 1938 dollars. Me, I was just glad that the new schoolhouse was already built. I doubt we could have had a second miracle.

Fall

One day in late 1938, the party line was ringing a bit more than usual. Word was getting around that the famous Saturday Evening Post illustrator, Norman Rockwell, had bought property in Arlington to use as a summer residence for his family. Being a boy of eight, such news was unimportant to me. I was busy fishing and hunting, and I wasn't much interested in reading the Saturday Evening Post.

1939

Sunday, May 28th

On Sunday, May 21st, my Aunt Amy turned eighteen; and one week later, on Sunday, May 28th, she and Bob eloped. They had been sweet on one another for the three years Bob had lived with us, and once Amy was of age, they decided it was time to get married. Everyone was excited and my grandmother even gave them three acres of land as a wedding present. They built a house on it with their own hands, and they still live there, seventy years later. I think I was more excited than anyone else, because now it was official that Bob was a member of the family, even if in our view he already was.

Spring

My dad's life as a farmer was, by definition, unpredictable. Weather, pestilence, disease, the economy, and even world events all impacted our land and how we survived. In the 1920s, my dad had lost his entire herd when the floor of our barn caved in, trapping the animals and condemning them to death. It was an incredible blow financially that took years to recover.

One Spring morning some official-looking men had approached the barn and talked intently to my father. They spent quite a bit of time with the cattle and later I learned that they had been inspecting the cows and had tested them for the cattle disease Brucillosis. My dad anxiously awaited the results of the test, knowing that the cows which tested positive would be destroyed in a statewide effort to curb the disease.

A few weeks later, my dad got the news that every cow except one heifer, Betsy, had tested positive. My dad and Bob had to take all of the others to the slaughterhouse to be put down. He was paid just thirty-nine dollars per head for each of the cows we lost, nothing compared to what they had cost and the ongoing value they provided us.

Losing a herd once was devastating enough; losing it twice in less than fifteen years was almost too much to bear, and financially brought us to the edge of total ruin. There were no regular milk checks coming in, and my dad had to make a tough call about how to continue to support the family. Soon after his herd was wiped out, he swallowed his pride and went to town to sign up for FDR's New Deal program, the Works Progress Administration, commonly known as the WPA.

The first day my dad showed up for work, he was shocked at how many men were sitting around, doing nothing, and collecting a paycheck to do it. Men stood leaning on their shovels, talking and laughing, as my dad broke his back digging. Then, after doing practically zero all morning, everyone else stopped for an entire hour to have lunch, before going back to leaning and talking some more. My dad, on the other hand, quickly ate the lunch my mother had packed for him in his lunch bucket and got back to his shovel. At the end of the day, he got the same amount of money as the other guys had, but the difference was he had *earned* his pay. Disgusted and discouraged, he quit the WPA after just one day.

The next morning, my dad hooked up our horse team, Dick and Prince, and approached the road crew up on Sandgate Road and offered to hire out himself and his team of two horses for five dollars per day. The crew was trying to fortify the road that had been torn apart from the Great New England Hurricane. On a handshake, dad began work hauling logs and he helped to build a dike to protect the road from any flooding that future weather disasters might bring.

Summer

I don't exactly remember when or how I first heard that the Rockwell family had officially arrived in town, but somewhere along the way I learned that they had moved into a farmhouse about three miles up the road from us. Bert Immen, the real estate agent in town, had sold them a farm with about sixty acres and some of the local folks had worked on fixing it up, including making one of the two barns into a studio for Mr. Rockwell to work. From all accounts, he and his wife were nice people, even if they were city folks.

CHAPTER THREE
WEST ARLINGTON, VERMONT
1940 - 1942

1940

Late Fall

News quickly spread that the Arlington High School had burned down to the ground. No one was hurt, but classes had to be temporarily set up at a local inn. Folks shook their heads and clucked over how unlucky our town could be to have lost two schools in such a short amount of time. Decisions had to be made what to do – to rebuild a new high school or to bus the kids to other local schools – and a special town meeting was called. Vermont is famous for its town meetings, and with matters of such local importance, a consensus has always been sought to make the decision that suits the citizens the best.

1941

Monday, January 20th

The temperature had dropped into the single digits earlier that day and more snow was on its way. After dinner, my grandmother, parents, Edith, and I went into our parlor and I filled the woodstove one last time for the night. My grandmother sat in the corner chair as she always did; my dad and mom sat on either side of Edith on the sofa; and I sat on the floor by the woodstove. Joy and Ardis were on the floor playing, throwing a small red ball in the air and swooping up as many of the scattered six-pointed jacks as they could, laughing when the ball rolled out of their hands.

Looking at his watch, my father crossed to the console hi-fi and turned on the radio. In a few minutes, the familiar sound of President Roosevelt's voice boomed through our radio, giving his Third Inaugural Address. As Joy and Ardis played, the rest of us sat still, leaning toward the radio and listening intently. I was almost eleven years old in age, but I was beyond my years in many ways. As the second "man" on the farm, I had had to grow up fast, and I was well aware of how important this radio address was going to be.

The entire world was on edge, and so was everyone in our parlor. Across the Atlantic, Hitler had conquered much of Europe. France had fallen six months before, along with Denmark, Norway, The Netherlands, Luxembourg, and Belgium. Mussolini had joined Hitler's side. There were limited reports of Jews being rounded up and put in camps by the thousands. Bombing raids on London and other cities had become a nightly occurrence. In the Pacific, Japan's threat was growing. The questions on everyone's mind that night were simple, but we knew the answers would not be: Would we enter the war? If so, when? How? And, what would it take to stop Hitler? Japan?

As FDR spoke, he tried to inspire us as a nation. He spoke of democracy. He spoke of the American spirit. He spoke of the faith of the country. And he spoke of the *privilege* of freedom. Two weeks earlier, FDR had eloquently given his State of the Union address before Congress and had put it in even more concrete terms in what would later come to be called the "four freedoms speech." He had said that the four essential human freedoms were freedom of speech; freedom of worship; freedom from want; and freedom from fear.

In both addresses to the American people, the ongoing theme from our President was that we had to believe in the strength of our will; and we had to support the strength of our beliefs. The speech was over fairly quickly, and everyone headed upstairs to bed.

That night, thinking about what FDR had said must have hit home, because I went to sleep with a feeling of pride in our nation; trust in our leader; and a strong belief in our way of life.

Early February

The town hall was lined wall-to-wall as a heated debate raged about whether or not to build the new high school. While most folks felt it should be rebuilt, for whatever reason, my dad wasn't one of them. He felt strongly that the students in the high school should be bussed to other local schools instead. My dad was no shrinking violet and as he stood up at the meeting waiting for his turn to be recognized, folks quieted and turned to hear what he would say. A widely respected man in the community, he held everyone's full attention as he passionately outlined his minority position. Finishing with thanks and a nod of his head, he sat down; and then the townspeople voted to build the new school.

March

When the weather starts to warm up, but the nights are still cold, the sap in maple trees starts to flow. That can only mean one thing – it's sugaring time!

We had plenty of maple trees on our wood lot and each year we produced about four hundred gallons of syrup. The whole family took part in sugaring. My dad bored tap holes in the trees with an auger and then everyone worked to insert spouts into the tap holes. After the spout was secure, we hung a bucket to collect the sap. When the buckets were full, we gathered the sap in a large tank which was placed on a wooden sled pulled by our team of horses, Dick and Prince. Then, we hauled the tank to our sap house, a small building in the woods. Inside, we dumped the sap into big storage tanks, and from the storage tank, the sap flowed down into an evaporator that boiled the water out of it. Our evaporator was fueled from good wood, courtesy of the barn behind the Otis property next door. It had been falling apart, and one day my dad and Bob finally tore it all the way down. When the evaporator heated up, big clouds of steam would rise up and out of the sap house. The end result was pure Vermont maple syrup.

When folks coming down Route 313 saw steam rising from our property, they knew the Edgerton's sap house was open for business. It was an important part of the farm's financial planning. The revenue from the maple syrup provided cash for seed for the coming season and also helped to get caught up on back bills.

Maple syrup time was also a social occasion, and many times we would have dozens of people coming by the sap house to buy syrup or just to take a taste in the shot glasses we kept just for that purpose. Sometimes we boiled eggs in the syrup instead of in water for a sweet tasting egg like none other. Another famous artist in town, Jack Atherton, designed the label that we put on our maple syrup containers, "Covered Bridge Farm."

Life on the farm was always sweet, but at sugaring time, it was just a bit sweeter.

Summer

We still hadn't financially recovered from losing our herd, so – ironically - my dad got work on the construction site of the new Arlington High School that he hadn't wanted built. He was hired as a laborer at seventy-five cents per hour for an eight-hour day, but was immediately promoted to the carpenter in charge and got a raise to ninety cents per hour. That extra $1.20 per day made a big, big difference.

Because the high school was being completed on a fast track, laborers from all around the state were coming to the area to work, but there were not enough rooms to house them. Seizing an opportunity, we took in many of the workers as boarders. We had two rooms available since Amy and Bob got married, plus rooms in the summer annex. Between my dad's work and the boarders, somehow we scraped by.

It wasn't all work, though. In the summertime, beginning the first Saturday of June each year and continuing until the last Saturday before Labor Day, the Grange held square dances at the pavilion behind the Grange Hall. The dances started at 8:00 p.m. and ended at midnight sharp because of Vermont's Blue Laws and also because the dances were held on church grounds. They were the social highlight of the summer, a weekly chance to get together and relax with friends, or welcome new folks to town.

The anticipation started each Saturday afternoon. You could feel the air charged with excitement as everyone hurried just a bit to get their chores done. Then, around 6:30 p.m., cars started driving over the covered bridge and parking on the Green just a hundred yards in front of our house. Dozens more lined the road to – and on - the covered bridge, leaving walking room for those crossing on foot. As the sun set, a local five-piece band played foot stomping music and the Caller stood with microphone in hand, shouting square dancing directions to the laughing folks on the dance floor. Kids ran in and out of the sea of parked cars, playing hide-and-seek. A concession stand was set up in the Grange Hall that served hot dogs, coffee, and cold soda. The air was filled with music and merriment, and when it finally was time to leave more than one dad carried a sleeping child home in his arms.

The Rockwells had made the decision to live year round in Arlington and they had jumped into the local goings on enthusiastically. They joined the Grange and that summer took turns helping out at the square dances, just like everyone else. More often than not, Norman swept the floor, tossing in corn meal to wax it, or he stood at the door and took tickets, greeting each person by name, warmly introducing himself as "Norman" and his wife as "Mary" to those he had not yet met.

It was at one of the Grange dances that summer that Norman asked my dad if he would pose for him the first time. Norman was creating a series for the Saturday Evening Post about a young soldier, and he needed some local men to be models. Norman had already spoken to Bobby Buck about being the main soldier, and in addition to Bobby and my dad, that night Norman recruited Jessie Watson, Frank White, Gene Pelham, and Pete Hebert. The deal Norman presented was too good to pass up – five dollars' pay for a few hours' work, just standing and making various faces and poses while Norman made sketches of what he saw.

On the agreed upon day, right on time, all six men showed up at Norman's Arlington studio located in the barn in front of his house. The end result was the first illustration of what came to be known as the Willie Gillis series, "Willie Gillis – Food Package." Mary came up with the main character's name, based on the children's book, *Wee Willie Winkie* that she had recently read to her sons.

In "Food Package," my dad appears twice. In the illustration you can see Bobby as Willie in the front; Jessie Watson in uniform over Bobby's right shoulder; my dad (in denim) over Bobby's left shoulder; Frank White behind Jessie Watson (also in denim); Gene Pelham, in uniform, behind my dad; Pete Hebert, barely visible with his right eye behind my dad; and my dad again, in the back of the gang. Norman chose to put my dad and Jessie in denim because the men were portraying early draftees/enlistees. At that time, the Army couldn't keep up with the demand for uniforms because there were so many men coming into the Army, so the early soldiers were given denim outfits instead.

Jessie Watson was our local game warden. If you look at his hand in the illustration, you'll notice he doesn't have an index finger. In real life, Jessie didn't have a finger, so that's exactly how Norman painted him. Frank was a laborer who did carpentry work, oftentimes for Walt Squires. Pete was a bit of a mystery man. No one knew much about him, but he was always willing to give folks a hand. Gene Pelham was a local illustrator for the Saturday Evening Post, too. He was also a wonderful photographer, and knew his way around an artist's studio, so soon he began photographing all of the models for Norman's Arlington illustrations.

Knowing my dad, I suspect he initially agreed to model for Norman because we needed every penny to get by, and it was a good way to help the family. But it's also true that my dad would never have offended Norman by saying no, Norman was just about as nice a guy as you could possibly be. And, it was an honor for Norman to choose my dad to be in the Willie Gillis series, it was a way my dad could help the war effort, too.

Monday, December 8th

Everyone in the house gathered around the radio, somber and intent. The President of the United States was about to address the nation:

"Yesterday, December 7, 1941, a day which will live in infamy, the United States of America was suddenly and deliberately attacked by naval and air forces of the Empire of Japan…"

With those thirty words, President Roosevelt began a speech that ended with informing our country that we had declared war against Japan. There were no more words necessary than that.

1942

Winter

Following our official declaration of war against Japan, Germany declared war on the United States. Norman wanted to do something for the entire war effort since he was too old to fight, so he decided to create some illustrations that might help the cause. After mulling over how or what he might use, he turned to the Four Freedoms Proclamation in FDR's State of the Union Address for inspiration.

Norman's idea generally was brilliant, but even though he finally knew *what* he wanted to illustrate, he continued to struggle with *how* to capture the essence of the four freedoms in an illustration. All of his ideas seemed to be lacking something, and he was unhappy that he couldn't grasp just the right image to make it work. But then, Norman was always a bit unhappy with his work. That's the way he was.

June

Norman himself used to tell the story that one night in the darkness after midnight, he had bolted upright in bed and thought about my father – and he was so excited at the thought, he wanted to call his best friend, Mead Schaeffer, another *Post* illustrator who had moved with his wife, Elizabeth, to Arlington just a year before. And he would have called, Mead, too, except that he didn't want to disturb all the other folks along Mead's party line.

The thought that had energized him in the night was the image of seeing my father more than a year before, as my dad had stood up in the town meeting to debate whether or not the Arlington High School – the very school I would be attending in just a few short months – should be rebuilt after burning down. Norman, a relative newcomer to Arlington at the time, had attended the meeting because it would have an influence on the schooling of his own three sons, Jarvis (we called him Jerry), Tommy, and Peter. But now, in the middle of the night, with the issue of to build or not to build long gone, the memory of how everyone in that room had listened to my father, his passion, his eloquence, and his minority point of view with such respect and appreciation, struck the creative chord in Norman that set off a firestorm of inspiration. *This* was freedom of speech; and *this* was what America was all about.

September

I was finally in seventh grade! In a brand new school! The new school had three wings – one for fifth and sixth graders; one for seventh and eighth; and the main area for ninth through twelfth grades. It was a beautiful school, and a far cry from where we had gone before, with large classrooms, huge chalkboards up front on the wall, and plenty of brand new desks. But while our new school had many wonderful things, one thing it did *not* have was a working cafeteria, so when the weather was nice, we were allowed to eat our lunches outside.

September brought a lot of eating-lunch-outside days. We would all wait patiently for our teacher, Mrs. Mabel Cullinan, to indicate whether we would eat in or out. Mrs. Cullinan was a no-nonsense woman in her forties with sharp facial features framed by shoulder-length dark hair sprinkled with gray. She was an ample woman who never wore make-up and was always modest in her dress. She was also a tough disciplinarian, who had firm control over the twenty-five students in her classroom, half of them boys, half girls. Yep, Mrs. Cullinan was a good teacher, but she also could look over the top of her glasses and with one intense glare silence a room.

One day early in the year I was so hungry waiting for lunch, I thought I'd pass out. I must have been going through one of those growth spurts like you do when you're a boy, almost a teen. Fifteen minutes before the lunch bell. My stomach was growling. Ten minutes. The growling got so loud I thought sure someone would hear it. Five minutes. I couldn't concentrate on my math problems, I wanted to eat! Finally, Mrs. Cullinan looked up from her desk and glanced outside, debating.

Two minutes. I thought about sneaking the apple from my lunch bucket and somehow getting at least one bite into my mouth when she wasn't looking, but I was afraid of getting in trouble. I was, after all, now at the high school.

One minute until the bell. Slowly, she said, "You can eat outdoors today. Be sure to pick up your trash and bring it in to throw away. Class dismissed."

My best friends were Leo Budro, Don Brown, Charlie Gould,

and Kenny Smith. The five of us practically ran out the door to the fresh mountain air and sunshine; staked out a place under a huge maple tree; and sat in a semi-circle, pooling our food in the middle. I had a big lunch bucket, like the kind the old railroad workers had, our family didn't have money to waste on paper lunch bags.

I think it's fair to say that my sisters and I always had just about the best lunches of anyone at school, being from a farm. September meant sandwiches full of slices of huge, fresh tomatoes sprinkled with brown sugar; other months we had fresh fruits and vegetables along with the standard peanut butter and jelly or baloney sandwiches. I didn't mind sharing most of the time, but I was so hungry that day, I ate all of my lunch and half of Kenny's.

After wolfing down lunch, we walked around the schoolyard a bit, then headed back to the school. The trees hadn't quite peaked in their autumn color, but soon the Valley would be blanketed in brilliant oranges, reds, and yellows. As we filed back into our classroom, the girls moved to their desks slowly, giggling and whispering as they glanced over at my friends and me. We couldn't hear what they were saying, but we were pretty sure we didn't want to know. Most girls at that age were silly, other than maybe Janet Cross. I happened to look up just then and saw Janet smiling at me. She looked at me kinda…strange. I felt myself freeze for just a moment, before awkwardly nodding my head and then quickly turning my attention to Mrs. Cullinan, who had patiently cautioned us to take our seats and prepare for our afternoon lessons. I had known Janet since first grade, and she seemed more like one of the guys. She was pretty neat as girls went, a good athlete and she liked the outdoors, which made her ok by me. Still, she was a girl, and I didn't have much time or interest for girls. Life for me was farming, hunting, fishing, school, and sports. I was too busy to think of much else.

Toward the end of the afternoon, I was daydreaming in class. Suddenly, there was a loud knock on our classroom door. I jumped in my seat, startled at the noise, realizing my mind had been wandering, and wondering if Mrs. Cullinan had noticed I wasn't listening to her lecture. I guess she didn't, because she was looking toward the door as it opened and our principal, Mr. Moore, poked his head in.

Mr. Moore was medium in size, almost bald and physically strong, and he cared about his students very much. He was a carpenter on the side, and appreciated hard work. The carpentry work and building ultimately took him from school administration many years later, when he started his own construction company. He was well-liked by the students because in addition to being tough, he was fair.

"I need to see James for a minute, please," he said to Mrs. Cullinan.

The whole class let out a long "Ooooooo!" sound and my heart stopped. Was I in trouble? Had he known I wasn't paying attention? Was there an emergency at home? I sat there, frozen.

Mrs. Cullinan's voice boomed, "James Edgerton! Close your book and go with Mr. Moore."

I did as I was told and slowly got up from my desk. Mr. Moore and I walked silently down the hall. No talking was ever allowed in the halls when classes were in session, so that the students weren't disturbed. It seemed like it took forever to walk to the Principal's office, even though it was probably only a few minutes. Mr. Moore stopped by his secretary's desk and told me to go into his office and take a seat.

I slowly walked into Mr. Moore's office and looked around. There was a big desk and an even bigger chair behind the desk. A framed degree hung on the wall, next to a clock with a huge pendulum that swung back and forth loudly. A plant sat in the window that looked like it needed watering, and books neatly lined a shelf in a corner of the room. As I squinted my eyes to see the titles, Mr. Moore came through the door, and I jumped for the second time that day.

"Take a seat, James, take a seat," he said quickly, pointing to a smaller chair in front of the desk.

I sat down on the edge of the chair, so that I could keep my feet flat on the floor to keep my knees from shaking. I didn't know what to do with my hands, they seemed to just hang over the sides of the chair, so I put them in my lap, and waited for Mr. Moore to speak.

"James, Mrs. Cullinan has been talking to me about your progress in her class this year and I wanted to talk to you about that."

My heart went into high gear when he said that. I was wondering what I had done wrong, waiting for the boom to drop. I thought about how I was going to tell my mom and dad that I had been called into the Principal's office and what punishment I was going to get. Edgertons didn't get in trouble, you did the right thing. My stomach started to feel all tied up inside and my hands felt like lead weights just sitting in my lap.

"She tells me that you are quite a good student. One of the best in the class in just about every subject, actually."

"*What?*" I thought in my head as he kept talking.

"…because Mrs. Cullinan thinks, and I agree, that you have the ability to be successful in your school career and maybe to do more than farm – not that there's anything wrong with farming, mind you, but I just wanted to tell you, well, keep up the good work." And with that, he dismissed me back to my class.

By the time I made my way back to Mrs. Cullinan's, school was pretty much over, so everyone was gathering up their books and jackets to head home. My friends looked up at me when I walked in to make sure I was ok and that Mr. Moore hadn't taken me to the boiler room, a not-uncommon occurrence for high-spirited boys in our school. I nodded, letting them know I was alright, then focused on gathering my gear. Mumbling "see ya later," I ran out the door, leaving my friends standing there, scratching their heads.

Sunday, October 11th

It was late afternoon and Fall was in full swing. The air was filled with the scent of my mother's apple pies and burning leaves, and the pumpkins we had picked from our garden and carved the night before stood outside the front door, smiling crookedly. Edith and Joy were hanging long rows of sheets on the clothesline out back. I could hear their voices once in a while when the wind shifted, even if I couldn't make out what they were saying.

Earlier in the day I had hunted squirrel and partridges, and in the next few weeks would start to trap muskrat and skunk. You could get a couple of bucks for a good muskrat pelt, two-to-three dollars for skunk pelts, a bit more if the skunk pelt were more black than white. Raccoon pelts also brought a few dollars. I ran a trap line with six to eight traps, using apple pieces on sticks above the traps as bait. Once the trap was sprung, the animals died quickly. I skinned them and then stretched the skins, letting them dry out for months, and then I'd sell the pelts in winter.

My dad was in the barn and I was busy working in the field when I heard a noise, so I looked up and what I saw made me stop cold: A man, a woman, and three young boys were riding brand new, shiny-red bicycles down the country road that ran in front of our farmhouse. I couldn't believe it! We had one old, used boy's bike that my three sisters and I shared, but these were all brand new bikes! I just stood there with the rake in my hand, my mouth wide open. Then, suddenly, the man saw me and he smiled and raised his hand in greeting, before they all pedaled out of sight. I was too shocked to raise my hand in reply, and I just stood there, until I heard my dad calling to me from in front of the barn.

"Buddy! Get going! There's not much daylight left!" he shouted.

"Yes sir!" I shouted back, as I continued looking down the road absently, leaning on my rake, still wondering who the heck those people were, "yes, sir."

Early November

I had turned twelve in March and it was time I took my place on the farm as a man. With Bob married and making his own way, my grandfather and Uncle Charlie passed, and not as many day laborers coming by – a lot of men had enlisted to protect our country in the war – my dad needed me all the more. Stan still helped out when he could, but he was a senior in high school that year and was pretty active, so he didn't have as much time for chores, plus the tourist home partnership next door was falling apart and it was becoming obvious that Stan would not be our neighbor for long.

November brought with it the need to prepare for the winter that was just about upon us. One of the most important chores at that time of year was to cut the wood we would need for the woodstoves to last us through the cold months. Cutting wood was a dangerous job and the responsibility of doing it right – and, more important, safely – was a heavy one. It was the first real "man's job" a son undertook in the hierarchy of farming.

Dad hitched up Dick and Prince to our bobsled, a wide wooden surface on two runners, and we trudged up to our woodlot. I carefully carried the two-man cross-cut saw, a long ragged blade with two well-worn wooden handles on each end. My dad led the team through the lot and he stopped at a dead tree precariously leaning against another tall healthy tree right beside it.

"Stand over there, Buddy," he said, motioning to the other side of the dead tree, "and give me the other end of the saw." I did as I was told and took my place.

"Now, spread your legs apart and get your balance, then place the middle of the blade against the bark of the tree and pull it toward you with your arms, don't use your legs, keep them planted hard and bend your knees."

I pulled it back and the blade jerked, it seemed to jump away from the bark by itself.

"Try again, Buddy. This time, press a little bit against the tree as you pull it back, let the teeth grip the bark."

I felt the jagged metal cut through the bark and the blade did not meet much resistance. When I had pulled the full length of the blade, my elbows ended up bent, high behind me, and I was leaning backwards at the same time my dad had leaned forward, his arms fully extended.

"Now, I'm going to pull back, and let me do the work, you just guide *your* end and keep the pressure of the blade against the tree. Keep your feet where they are and bend at the waist."

With almost no effort, my dad pulled on the saw and it flew back to him so fast, I had to hold onto my handle to keep from losing my balance. He smiled and nodded, and I pulled my end again, and then we started pushing and pulling the blade in a rhythm that worked its magic against the bark of the tree. Soon, the cut was so deep that the tree crashed to the ground. We laid the saw against another tree so as not to accidentally step on it, and my dad and I dragged the felled tree over to the sled. For hours, we spotted a tree, lined ourselves up, took a stance, and cut. When we ran out of dead trees, we picked live trees. When the sled was full, we bound the logs with chains and binders and bobbed the load down the mountain.

"Good job, Buddy," my father said over his shoulder without looking, as he led the team and I followed behind.

My shoulders were already sore, but it felt good knowing I had crossed more than just the property line of our woodlot.

CHAPTER FOUR
WEST ARLINGTON, VERMONT
1943

January

After six long months, Norman Rockwell had finished his Four Freedom portraits. Before shipping them off to his editor, Ben Hibbs, at the Saturday Evening Post, Norman framed them and put them on display at the West Arlington Grange. Folks from all over the area came to see the paintings, which stood massively along the wall, each one measuring an amazing 45 ¾" tall by 35 ½" wide, except for Freedom of Worship, which measured slightly larger at 46" by 35 ½". I don't know why that is, but that's the truth.

I walked into the Grange Hall and took my place in line among our neighbors. Everyone in the room was hushed in awe by what stood before us. First in line was Freedom of Speech. I easily recognized Carl Hess standing up at the meeting, just like my dad had. Carl was a bit younger than my dad and owned a one-pump gas station across the way, on the other side of the river. He was a regular grease monkey, the hard working son of a German immigrant, Henry Hess. Through marriage, the Hess family is kin to the Edgertons – my Aunt Elizabeth, Mom's baby sister, married Henry's son, Lawrie.

I spoke with Carl's son, George, one time about the connection between the Edgertons and the Hess families, including our connection through the Freedom of Speech illustration. He told me that the leather jacket that his dad had worn in Freedom of Speech had originally been Gene Pelham's, but that somehow his dad had ended up with it. He wasn't sure how it happened, but that's what his dad had told him. The leather jacket had sat around the Hess gas station for a long time before they ultimately cut it up to use as grease rags. It was the only time Norman had used Carl for an illustration (at the suggestion of Gene Pelham), though Carl later posed for Don Spaulding's Lone Ranger comic book covers just like me, and some Buck Jones comic book covers, too. Don was a student of Norman's, but I'll tell you about that later.

Other neighbors from town peered down from the massive Freedom of Speech illustration hanging in the Grange Hall. In the lower right corner, Jim Martin was looking back over his shoulder at Carl. Seemed funny to see Jim in a suit, he was a skilled carpenter who worked with local builder Cliff Wilcox and sometimes Walt Squires, another model Norman frequently used. Norman loved to use Jim as a model, he had a great face and his hands were calloused from years of hard work. Jim was, more often than not, in work clothes, though I'm sure he would have put a tie on to go to a town meeting.

Harry Brown sits above Jim, and Bob Benedict, Sr. is to the left of Carl. Peeking out from behind Bob is Rose Hoyt, one of Norman's all time favorite Arlington models. She was thirty-three years old when she posed for Freedom of Religion. Rose's life wasn't easy. She had ten kids, eight boys and two girls. It seemed like about once a year she and her husband, Cyril, would have another child, and they worked hard to support their large family. They lived uptown, and in high school I played basketball with two of the Hoyt boys. Rose was truly a sweet person. She lived to be ninety-five years old, and Cyril lived to be eighty-nine.

The next illustration on display was Freedom of Worship. The story goes that the phrase, "Each according to the dictates of his own conscience," was given to Norman by Mary, who had read it in one of her many books, but neither he nor Mary could ever find the source. Mrs. Harrington is the older lady in the illustration. She was a widow and she lived alone about a half mile above Bob and Amy, up on River Road. I never knew her husband or much about her, but the wife of her son, Jesse, is in Norman's "The Gossips." Win Secoy, near the center, was an uptown plumber. In those days, there wasn't much need for a plumber around town, but he was a good handyman, too, and he kept himself busy. Jim Martin was in this illustration, too. As a matter of fact, he was the only model who appeared in all four of the Four Freedom illustrations, it's his face in the lower right corner of Freedom From Want and as the father in Freedom From Fear.

Freedom From Want had Norman and Mary's cook, Mrs. Wheaton, front and center. By all accounts, the story goes that she cooked the turkey in the illustration and then the Rockwells ate it. Mrs. Wheaton's husband, Thaddeus, is in it, too. Lester Brush, whose hair is visible on the right just above Florence

Lindsey's big smile, was the son of a local Episcopalian priest. He was about six foot seven inches, and weighed in not much more than a hundred fifty pounds dripping wet – "a tall drink of water," as my dad used to say. His brother, Larry, is the father in "Visit To A Country Doctor" illustration, but the third Brush brother was never used. Two of our Hoisington neighbors are in Freedom From Want –Shirley and her brother Billy, who later became a realtor in Bennington. Charlie Lindsey and his daughter Florence are another family featured in Freedom From Want.

The line slowly moved toward the fourth illustration, Freedom From Fear. I looked up at the illustration and searched for familiar faces once more. There was Jim Martin, again, with Dorothy Lawrence as the mom. Walt Squires' kids, Marjorie and David, were the boy and girl in bed. Marjorie was just eight years old and David five when they modeled for Freedom From Fear. Marjorie later told me Norman said, "Keep your eyes closed and lie quiet," as Gene Pelham snapped pictures of the sleeping children. They pretended to sleep in a bed that sat in the upstairs of Norman's first Arlington studio, Marjorie's own rag doll is on the floor.

The Squires were the closest neighbors to the Rockwells at their first home in Arlington, and Norman frequently used the Squires as models. They were also friends. After Marjorie's mom had surgery, Norman offered to have his cook take care of the family's meals for two weeks. Mary came by and read *The Hobbit* to her mother as she recuperated, and years later, after moving to Stockbridge, Mary came all the way to Arlington to visit Marjorie's mother when she took seriously ill again. Norman even left his family's bikes for the Squire children to use when the Rockwells went on vacation; Norman had taught Marjorie to ride her first two-wheeler. Why would Norman do that?

"That's just the way he was," Marjorie would later smile.

February

The Four Freedoms were published as inserts to the Saturday Evening Post in four successive weekly issues beginning February 20th. Each illustration was accompanied by an essay written by an influential author of the time: Booth Tarkington, a Pulitzer Prize writer, wrote the accompanying text for Freedom of Speech. Famous historian Will Durant supplied his thoughts for Freedom of Worship. A Filipino immigrant named Carlos Bulosan wrote the essay for Freedom from Want, and Stephen Vincent Benét, a staff member of the Office of War Information ("OWI") and poet in his own right, wrote eloquently for the Freedom from Fear edition. Post readers ordered twenty-five thousand copies of the set of four posters, and the OWI ordered two and a half million copies. Norman was pretty proud of that, though he didn't talk about it much, because the OWI had rejected his sketches and his offer to help the previous year.

Next came a war bond drive with the Four Freedoms at the center. A tour of the paintings went through the whole country, and it was amazing. When all was said and done, Norman's Four Freedoms were seen by more than a million people, and they had raised more than one hundred thirty-three million dollars in war bonds. Even President Roosevelt acknowledged Norman's accomplishment, writing him a personal letter, which read: "I think you have done a superb job in bringing home to the plain, everyday citizen the plain, everyday truths behind the 'Four Freedoms.'" Norman didn't have the letter sitting out or framed or anything, the way most folks would probably do if they got a personal letter from the President of the United States. As a matter of fact he never even mentioned it to us, which doesn't really surprise me knowing Norman. I read about that letter once in a story about Norman, and I'm sure it's true.

In West Arlington, while we were excited to be a part of something so special, no one much talked about it. Looking back, *we* were the "plain, everyday citizens" President Roosevelt wrote about, but to us it wasn't special, it was just – normal. To tell you the truth, though, years later when I learned about my dad's large role in Norman's inspiration for Freedom of Speech, which led to the idea for the other three freedoms, I couldn't help but feel pretty proud that my dad had been a part of something truly great.

Spring

In a town the size of Arlington, small events or large - didn't matter which - automatically became big news. Like mile markers in the road, that's how folks kept track of the years: "The Great Flood of 1936 - you know, the worst flood of the century!" and, "[T]he fall of 1940 – you know, when the high school burned down," and so forth. It was comforting in an odd sort of way to connect the dots of life's ups and downs as we endlessly worked, season after season. And perhaps no event was more talked about for years than the Spring of 1943, when the studio in front of the Rockwell's Arlington house burned to the ground.

I didn't know the Rockwells very well then, just knew they lived up the road and that my dad had modeled for Norman, and that he was a nice man and famous artist. But after I got to know them, Tommy told me himself what happened the night of the fire.

Tommy and his brothers had been really sick with the measles. A few weeks before Tommy's tenth birthday, he had gotten up in the night sometime after midnight to get a drink and had seen flames pouring out of the studio. He ran to his parents' bedroom and banged on the door, frantically waking up Norman and Mary, then tore down the stairs to watch the fire out the window, his brothers sleepily following after him. Tommy thought all of the excitement was "cool," too young to understand the dangers that were close by, or the implications to his father's art work. Norman couldn't call the fire department because the phone lines were burned, so he drove to get help, leaving Mary and the kids in the house. By the time the fire department arrived, it was pretty much done. The show was over; the studio – and twenty-eight years of Norman's life as an artist - was gone.

Norman decided he wanted to stay along the banks of the Battenkill, and so shortly after the fire, he and Mary decided to buy a house. Within days of the fire, they bought the house next to ours. The "tourist home" idea had run its course, and the partnership between the Griffis and Devermans had ended, so the house was available immediately, making it ideal; plus, there were eight acres of land that could be used to build another studio. Rockwell would later say that one of the most compelling reasons for them to buy was the fact that the house was next door to my parents, well-thought of and well-respected people in West Arlington. With the two houses being so close together, the importance of who your neighbors were couldn't be overlooked.

The Rockwells moved into the house next door right away, and Norman arranged to use the one-room schoolhouse in the summer months until his own new studio could be built. I remember thinking the day they moved in that I couldn't believe how much stuff they had to put in the house. A big moving truck had backed up to the front door, which was flung open, and big, muscular men went back and forth time after time, in and out of the truck, carrying boxes and furniture and rugs – and toys. I had been working in the field and had walked around the front of the house to take a break – and, to be perfectly honest, to check out the new neighbors a little more closely. I was sad that Stan wouldn't be next door, and I wondered what the Rockwells would be like. As I watched the movers, all of a sudden I let out a loud, "Ooohhh!" as I saw one of the men carrying a new, red, shiny – and familiar - bike under each of his arms.

Maybe living next door to the Rockwells wasn't going to be so bad, after all.

Mid-April

I think being the youngest child in a family has its advantages. First, everyone always thinks you're cute; second, no matter what you do that's impolite, people let you get away with it because you're cute. Third, you can walk up to new neighbors who have just moved in and introduce yourself without seeming silly – because you're cute.

"You children should go over and say hello," my mother had said the day after the moving truck was gone. "Buddy, you go over, the Rockwells have three sons and it would be nice if you went over and welcomed them as neighbors."

"I will," I said, thinking I didn't really want to. It was a nice day and I had plans to go fishing – alone. "Later, maybe."

"Well, you shouldn't wait any longer, it's not polite, we don't want our new neighbors to think we're rude."

"Then I think *you* should go over, Mom," I said, half kidding and half not, "you wouldn't want them to think *you're* rude."

"James A. Edgerton!" my mother said, "don't sass me! Now, take your sisters, and go over and say hello. I'm baking a pie and I'll be going over in a bit after I freshen up."

"Alright, alright," I said, getting up from the kitchen table, "but do I *have* to take the girls, too?"

"Yes," said my mother firmly, "and Buddy – tuck your shirt in and go comb your hair."

I went upstairs to my room and looked in the mirror and spit in my hands, then smoothed them over my hair quickly. I grabbed my fishing pole from the corner of my room and went down the stairs, calling after my sisters.

"Girls! Let's go!" I said, and headed out the door without waiting.

I heard the front door slam shut and Ardis came running up from behind me. Then she ran right past me, straight up to the Rockwell's front door. She knocked loudly and the door opened right away. By the time I arrived a minute later, Ardis was already standing in the Rockwell's parlor, chatting away to a woman and three boys.

"We're really glad you moved in because now we'll have kids next door to play with," Ardis was saying to the boys. "I have a brother and two sisters and we have a lot of fun. We have two horses and lots of cows and pigs and in the summertime we swim down at the Swimming Hole except Buddy because lots of time he goes off hunting or fishing by himself. But he's really nice, he's a really good baseball player and he and my dad work hard. My sister, Edith, is practically a grown-up, she's fourteen, so she doesn't play as much anymore, but she does like to go to the Swimming Hole…" and on and on she went, as I stood there without saying a word, my fishing pole in my hand. The woman looked at me over Ardis' head and smiled, and gently interrupted her.

"Why, this must be your big brother, Buddy. Buddy, I'm Mary, and these are my boys, Jerry, Tommy, and Peter."

One by one, the boys half looked up and mumbled hello and I lifted one hand in a kind of half wave, the way young boys do when they are forced to meet another kid. Jerry was the oldest. He was several inches shorter than I was and seemed to be a few years younger. He had a model airplane in his hands that he was fidgeting with while his mother talked. Peter was the youngest. He looked to be about seven or eight, and he was standing in front of his mother, leaning back against her, kind of shy. Tommy was the middle son. He was average in size, had a nice smile, and he was eyeing my fishing pole.

I remembered what my mother had said and wanted to show I was a good neighbor, so I said,

"I was going over to the river to fish a bit, if you want to come." It was more a statement than a question.

"Yeah, sure, that sounds good," said Tommy, with a slight lisp, suddenly smiling.

"Nah," said Jerry, looking down at his model, "maybe later though."

"Peter, you stay here, too," Mary said, "I don't want you going down to the river without a grown-up."

And with that, Tommy and I left, leaving Ardis to follow Mary around the house, chatting away.

"Boy, she sure talks a lot!" said Tommy, laughing, as we got outside and headed toward my secret, favorite fishing hole.

"You have no idea!" I said, laughing, thinking Tommy was A-ok.

Monday, May 24th

"Today's the day!" I thought, excitedly.

"Today's the day!" My heart sang as I made my way downstairs to breakfast.

"Today's the day!" I tried to calm my nerves as I ran out to the barn, my eyes darting everywhere, looking for my dad.

"Buddy, is that you?" my dad said as he entered the barn behind me.

"Yes, you're here! – I mean, I'm me – er, uh, *yes sir!*" I finally stammered.

"Grab the harness and let's go, Dick and Prince are waiting," he said over his shoulder, ignoring my inability to spit out two words together as he headed back out the door.

My heart was pounding as I reached up on the wall and took down the horses' harness. Quickly running out the door, I went over to my dad, where he stood beside our team. They seemed bigger today, taller, and I took a deep breath as I looked up at the pair.

"You know what to do?" my father asked.

"Yessir." I said.

"I hope so," I thought.

"You need my help?" my dad said, trying to sound casual.

"No sir, I don't think so, thanks," I said, trying hard to sound casual back.

"Alright, Buddy, then harness 'em up and let's go, we need to harrow the eight acre piece before the sun goes down."

I took a breath and eyed Dick and Prince as they stood, waiting patiently, and carefully straightened out the tangle of straps. I put a bit in each of their mouths, then put the harness collars around their necks and pulled the straps around their sides, and led them outside. As my dad watched, I hooked the team up to the spring-tooth harrow and then placed the steering straps from the horses behind it, leaving about fifteen to twenty feet of strap. And with that, my dad and I headed out to the top meadow, side-by-side, one grown man and one young man who had just gone through one of the most important rites of passage you could pass, all of it without a word from my father. But as we walked in silence, both of us staring ahead at some unknown spot in the meadow, he reached up and put his arm around me and softly patted my shoulder.

It was a mild day, and the sky was clear. It probably sounds a bit corny, but it was a great day to be out and working the land. I felt confident and strong, knowing I had my father's total trust and that I could now step up to the task of filling the void on the farm that Stan Deverman's leaving had created. My family needed me and I felt good about handling that responsibility, too. I was thirteen years old.

My dad headed up the ridge, leaving me alone with my thoughts and Dick and Prince. I had been harrowing the high meadow for about an hour when I heard a loud rumbling sound in the distance, down the Valley.

"Shoot," I thought, puzzled and listening intently, "sounds like thunder."

But as I stood there, the thunder didn't stop, it just got louder and louder and louder, echoing off the hills. Suddenly, a B17 Bomber roared practically over my head, flying right along the Battenkill River, just three hundred feet above the water. And as I watched, dumbstruck, it deeply tilted its wings in salute, then flew off, disappearing from our view as fast as it had appeared.

Uptown, Harry Becktoft - Elsie Deverman's husband, and brother-in-law to Art Deverman, our former neighbor - was standing outside of Mack Molding Company surrounded by a circle of co-workers as the B17 flew over the factory, ceremoniously tilting its wings to the crowd below.

"I wonder who that damn fool is?" laughed John Canfield, the shop foreman, looking up and shaking his head.

"That 'damn fool' is my son!" said Harry, as he swiftly charged John, ready to defend his son's honor with his fists. The men held Harry back as John apologized profusely, and then they all turned their attention back to Art, cheering loudly - for the proud father *and* for his twenty-three year old son who set his Flying Fortress in a sharp climb, up and out of the Valley, and headed to England with the Army Air Corp.

Over the next five months, Art would safely fly eight bombing raids over France and Germany before being shot down in broad daylight October eighth on a mission that cost the U.S. Army Air Corp forty bombers and countless men. Art and his surviving crew members were taken prisoner by the Germans and were placed in a POW camp at Mossburg, Germany, an international POW camp that had Russians, Serbs, Poles, and Americans. There wasn't much food at the camp, like many other POW camps, and he lost a lot of weight during the five hundred fifty-seven days he was a captive before being liberated by Patton on April 29, 1945. As it turns out, my Uncle Bob was with Patton's infantry on his famous march across Germany and liberated Barracks Two and Three at the POW camp. Art was in Barrack One. Though they were at the same POW camp on the same day, their paths did not cross. The next day, Art was set free and shipped to England before heading home to the states.

God bless the U.S. Army.

Early June

Within a very short time, Tommy and I had become very good friends. We explored the woods and the top pasture, and threw rocks from the covered bridge. I showed him around the farm and he helped me with my chores. My dad didn't mind having him around as long as the chores got done. Tommy seemed to like hanging out at our house, even though it wasn't as fancy as his. From the beginning, he often had dinner over with us.

"Boys, clear your dishes," said my mom as she got up from the table.

"Yes, ma'am," we said together.

When they first moved in, Norman wasn't around very much. Without a studio of his own, he had first arranged to share Mead Schaeffer's studio until summer, then he used the one-room schoolhouse during the summer months until he could get his studio built. One day, Tommy and I were headed toward the covered bridge when we saw his dad come out of the schoolhouse.

"Where ya going today, boys?" he asked as he came toward us.

"We're going jumping off the covered bridge!" said Tommy, excited. "There's a rope and everything, and Buddy's going to show me how to do it!"

"Be careful," Norman said, continuing to walk past us toward the house never even blinking an eye, "and have fun."

"We will!" I called after him as we walked.

"My dad likes you," Tommy said, smiling.

"I hope so," I replied.

Late June

Getting Norman's studio built was no easy task. First off, Norman needed a bulldozer for putting in the footings and clearing the land so the foundation could be laid. Unfortunately, there was only one bulldozer in the entire county at that time, at W.H. Daily & Sons, in Shaftsbury, because all of the others had been commissioned to help with the war effort. In order for the bulldozer to work, the ground had to have warmed up enough to have thawed, which meant waiting until early Spring. Then, when Norman needed it, so did everyone else. But the townsfolk tried to be accommodating to Norman, and finally the big equipment rumbled down River

Road and looped up behind the Rockwell house. I had never seen a bulldozer before, and I remember looking up and thinking that it was gigantic! I also thought it sure was going to speed things up a bit over doing everything by hand, like I was used to.

Norman hired Walt Squires to build the studio, and Walt brought in a crew for the project. Carpenters were paid one dollar per hour. Laborers were paid ninety cents per hour. As the men were busy starting work on the studio, Norman saw me in the field working and called me over to their yard.

"Buddy," he said smiling, his pipe in hand, "could you do me a favor? I hear that you're a strong young man and a good worker. Walt and the guys could sure use your help with building the studio, and I would appreciate it if you would. I'll pay you to do it, of course. How does seventy-five cents an hour sound?"

"Would I! Sure! Thanks, Norman!" I said, and I ran home to tell my mom the good news.

Seventy-five cents an hour! I couldn't believe it! I had never had an allowance before in my life, it was just expected that I would work on the farm doing my chores. And so there I was, Buddy Edgerton, a hard working young man who was willing to pick up stray nails, carry tools and lumber, or throw away trash, making almost as much as the grown men. It gave me just what I needed in pocket money to be able to do things with the Rockwell boys – go to the movies, get ice cream or cold sodas, or buy baseball cards. My family didn't have much extra money for fun things like that, and Norman – being Norman – had figured a way to let me have both my money and my pride, so that I could do things with his boys who were not poor like us.

My first job was to shovel a load of sand that had been dumped in Norman's front yard and move it into the backyard. I shoveled it into a wheelbarrow and carried it around between the houses and dumped it by the studio, then smoothed it over and over with a hand rake. It took a long time to get it done just right, but I wanted it to be perfect for Norman.

After the foundation was laid, Walt and the guys built the barn – a red, two-story workplace – pretty quick. Even though it was new, it blended right in, with a knotty pine exterior and a rustic interior to match. The main room was open to the second floor and had huge windows that reached from the floor to ceiling, allowing light to flood into the room for Norman to paint by. A built-in bench stretched below the window and built-in bookcases were on either side of the framed the wooden seat. Opposite the window, a fireplace made the room cozy; a kitchen and dark room were tucked behind the main room, and stairs led to the basement. To the right, stairs led up to another room that stored props, costumes, and supplies.

After the studio was finished, the landscaping had to be done. I helped the landscaper with the load of flagstone that Norman had ordered to make a path from the house to the studio. It had been delivered on our property by mistake. I carried the heavy flagstones, one at a time, from our driveway, across our yard and then into theirs and laid them in the ground, creating a perfect path for Norman. It took me days to do it, even if I was pretty strong, and when I was finished, I knew I had done a good job.

It was an exciting day at the Rockwell house *and* the Edgerton house when Norman's studio was finally finished. I felt like I had been part of something really important. Norman Rockwell's studio – well, it was practically sacred ground.

Summer

It was the first weekend after the studio was ready. Norman had walked in our back door late in the morning and had called to my mother. He needed to "borrow" me for a bit. When Norman told her what he had in mind, she agreed right away. I was in the barn with my dad when I heard my mother calling for me to come inside. As I ran toward the kitchen, I couldn't help but wonder what was important enough to take me from my chores.

When I got to the doorway, I noticed Norman was sitting at our kitchen table, talking to my mother, and he smiled as I walked in. I smiled back. I didn't get the connection, at first, that Norman had come for me, so I was surprised when he motioned to me to follow him, and called to my mother over his shoulder that we might be a while.

As we walked across the small strip of grass that separated our houses, Norman told me he needed me to model for a Boy Scout calendar illustration. That made me feel a little nervous, I had never modeled for anything in my life! But Norman made me feel better. He was real patient as he explained that all I had to do was wear a Boy Scout uniform, and he would tell me how to stand or what facial expression he wanted, while his photographer, Gene Pelham, took some pictures. That was it. For my time and help, I would earn five dollars. Five bucks for a few hours' work, same as my dad had gotten to model for Willie Gillis! Couldn't beat that.

We walked in the studio, and Norman crossed the room and

picked up a large box wrapped in brown paper. He opened the package and it was a brand new Boy Scout uniform. Norman handed it to me and I went in the bathroom to change. When I came out, Norman wrinkled up his forehead as he looked me over. He just stood there, quiet, and I kind of looked up at the ceiling, down at the floor, out the window. This modeling thing felt kinda weird, I wasn't sure what was expected of me at that moment, but I knew from the look on Norman's face that something clearly wasn't right.

After a few minutes of me just standing there, Norman took a long draw on his pipe.

"Looks a little big," he said quietly.

"Feels a little big," I replied.

"Looks a little new," he added.

"Feels a little new too, a little scratchy," I half-apologetically answered, sort of shrugging my shoulders.

"Hmmmm," said Norman, squinting his eyes.

"Hmmmm," I said, squinting my eyes back.

Then, all of a sudden, Norman's eyes lit up. He started walking to the door, grabbed his car keys, and motioned for me to follow. I had to practically run to keep up with Norman as we headed to his car.

"Climb in! We're going to the movies!" he cheerfully shouted over the roof of the car.

Wow, I thought, this modeling thing is pretty neat, after all! I get to walk around in a uniform, go to the movies, AND get paid five dollars! And, while I felt a little guilty that I had left my dad to cover my portion of the chores, it was nice to have a break from Saturday's work.

Norman carefully drove across the covered bridge and turned right onto Route 313. When we got to town, we parked the car and walked to the movie theatre. Norman asked to see the manager as I stood in the empty lobby, eyeing the popcorn left over from the night before. I hadn't eaten lunch before going to Norman's studio, and my stomach felt like it was going to growl any minute. I kept hoping it wouldn't, or hoping I could have some of that stale popcorn, one or the other.

Norman and the manager were talking and laughing for a few minutes. Then, they shook hands, and Norman motioned for me to come to his side, as the manager crossed the lobby. Norman pulled some change from his pocket and told me to go to the counter, where the manager was fixing a large bag of popcorn and two drinks, and then to come into the theatre. With that, Norman turned and went into the large auditorium.

I stood there for a minute as Norman left, and then turned and walked toward the counter. The manager was very nice, refusing to take the change I held out to him. He handed me the popcorn and drinks, and winked as he told me to enjoy the show.

Carefully balancing the popcorn in the crook of my arm, a drink in each hand, I somehow managed to open the door to the darkened theatre by catching the bottom of the door with my foot and quickly pulling it behind me, then immediately propping the door open with my elbow, squeezing my way inside. I was as careful as I could be, scared to death that I would spill something on the brand new Boy Scout uniform, and I was proud of myself when I didn't.

It took my eyes a few minutes to adjust to the change in light, and at first I couldn't see where Norman was. As a matter of fact,

I couldn't see much of anything at all. I blinked a few times and was finally able to make out shadows. As I peered through the darkness, I noticed that the theatre was completely empty except for Norman and another male figure. They both sat dead center in the middle of a row that was dead center in the middle of the auditorium. I walked down the side aisle on the left toward the row where they were sitting, and I remember that in the empty room my feet made a kind of slapping sound against the worn carpet that echoed. I had to hold back not to go faster and faster down the aisle. While I was carefully stepping sideways across the aisle toward a seat next to Norman, I noticed the man on the other side of Norman was none other than Gene Pelham, his camera balanced carefully on his knees. As soon as I sat down, the movie suddenly came on. It was "In Which We Serve," a blockbuster war movie written by Noel Coward that got two Oscar nominations. "Casablanca" beat it that year, but my favorite was always "In Which We Serve."

The story was about a British battleship, the HMS Torrin, that gets destroyed, and the men who cling to a life raft, waiting to be rescued. I don't remember all of the story, but one thing stands out in my mind almost seventy years later. The entire film, Norman sat quietly, like he was studying the movie, not just watching it. He didn't even seem to be watching the movie so much as he seemed to be watching the screen itself. During one particular scene, the warship filled the screen, and all of a sudden, Norman jumped up out of his seat and said, "That's it! That's it!" Gene aimed his camera at the screen and began clicking away at Norman's command.

The film immediately stopped and I turned around and looked toward the projection booth and saw the theatre manager looking down on us. He saw me looking and gave me a quick wave, before stopping the movie, rewinding the big reel by hand, and replaying the film until the ship appeared again. Then, the manager paused the movie right where the battleship was – he just stopped the whole movie! Norman began moving around the theatre to look at it from different places, standing still again, and the whole time he never said a word. After about five minutes of studying the ship, he called, "thank you!" to the manager, and waved to Gene and me to follow him out of the auditorium. Whatever Norman had come to the theatre to do, it was finished. I never did get to see the end of the movie.

Outside the theatre, Gene said good-bye and walked toward his car as we walked across the street to the local ice cream parlor, and Norman treated me to a double scoop of chocolate ice cream. I felt so special to be there with him, he had a way of making you feel like you really mattered, that you were important. He didn't rush me to finish my cone, even though I am pretty sure he was on a tight timetable and had a lot of thoughts on his mind about the ship. I smiled at the memory of going to the theatre – the manager had opened the entire theatre *just for him!* That was pretty amazing to a thirteen-year old boy.

Once we got in the car, Norman drove pretty quick back down 313 and pulled in the driveway behind the house. We got out of the car and he hurried back into the studio, I had to almost run again to keep up. Seemed every time we went somewhere that day, he was hurrying, except when he got me my ice cream.

When we got inside, Norman looked hard at me again, and this time I knew just to stand quietly, but he was making that funny face that said he still was not happy with my uniform.

"Buddy, go outside for a bit. Run around. Sit in the grass. Do what you would do in a Scout uniform. Then, come back in and let me take a look," said Norman.

I didn't have a clue what a boy in a Boy Scout uniform would do because I was never a Boy Scout. Yep, hate to tell it, but even though I ended up being the Boy Scout Norman illustrated most for their calendars, I never was one. Tommy and I went to a meeting one time, but all they did was have a treasure hunt, and it wasn't as interesting for us as exploring the back woods and hills behind our house on our own. Neither one of us ever went back.

I walked outside and stood there a minute, then started running around the yard a few times, feeling pretty silly. I think my mom saw me out our kitchen window, but if she did, she never came out. I sat on the ground and picked up a few handfuls of dirt and let them fall through my fingers, then got up and brushed off the seat of my pants. I stood there trying to figure out what else I could do and decided to climb a tree. Scouts probably climbed trees. I sat on the low branch of a maple in Norman's back yard, then climbed down. I had run out of ideas by then, so finally I walked over to the studio door and came in slowly. Norman was sitting down in front of his easel and Gene Pelham was sitting on the bench by the window, his big camera was on the bench beside him.

"Come on in, Buddy, stand over by Gene and let me take a look."

I did as I was told, and he smiled.

"Good. Now, stand over here," he motioned toward the studio door, "and look at me. Ok, don't smile, just be real serious, and now look up toward the ceiling."

I tried to be as serious as I could and stand as still as I could, even though my legs were itching from where I had sat in the grass.

"Ok, hold your hand up in a Scout salute and give me more eyes," he said patiently, so I lifted my brow and struggled to hold it.

"Perfect!" he said loudly as Gene finally began snapping the photos Norman needed.

After five minutes, I was through. Norman thanked me for my help, paid me my five dollars, putting it in a sealed envelope. As I turned to leave the studio he called after me.

"Buddy? Good job today," he said, smiling. "And you know something? You were the very first model I used in my new studio – how about that!"

"Thank you, sir" I said, too embarrassed to say more.

I flew home to tell my mother what had happened that afternoon, slowly leading up to the part about being Norman's very first model in his brand new studio. She smiled at me as I told her about my adventure. At the dinner table that night, my sisters made me tell the story all over again, especially the part about having the whole, entire movie theatre opened up just for us, and getting popcorn and a drink for free!

When the "I Will Do My Best" poster appeared on the Boy Scout calendar in 1945, I couldn't help but notice that the red kerchief I had modeled for Norman had become a beautiful, deep blue. When I asked him about it, he shrugged his shoulders and simply said, "The blue looked better. The red didn't really match the uniform." That's the way he was.

I knew I had been a part of something special that day, not

only modeling for the first time, but being the first model ever in Norman's new studio. I had witnessed the way he worked and his attention to detail, right down to wanting the uniform to look worn and wrinkled like it would if a boy had worn it a while. It was another milestone in my life. I was now part of a circle of people who could claim to have posed for a wonderful man, not just a wonderful artist.

The simple truth is, once you entered the world of Norman Rockwell, you never really left; you just happily co-existed from that point on. I have.

September

All of the townspeople in Arlington and West Arlington were jittery about the idea of the Germans coming down through Canada and invading the U.S. by marching south on Route 7 and right through our town. A journalist had written about this very possibility, and we just knew that the German bombers were going to head right for our covered bridge and bomb it into kingdom-come. In preparation for this disaster that we were told might be around the corner, our town formed a Civil Defense organization, and everyone had to be trained to be on the lookout just in case. So, the grown-ups and teenagers all took air raid spotting classes, learning how to identify the Messerschmitts from the Spitfires. We took turns acting out pretend invasions, and a plane spotting crew used walkie-talkies to act out the role playing.

Norman had been a part of the patriotic exercise, but he had messed up. He couldn't keep from laughing when Doc Russell got mad over the walkie-talkies because a Civil Defense worker wouldn't let him go over the bridge to deliver a baby since, in the pretend exercise, the bridge had been destroyed by the Krauts. Doc crossed the bridge anyway, and Norman got "reassigned" to work with my dad as his assistant. Put another way, Norman got fired.

My dad was the Chief of the West Arlington Volunteer Fire Department, and also was the Air Raid Warden. Norman was assigned to be my dad's Assistant Fire Department Chief – ironically, considering Norman's house had burned down – and that meant he was also the Assistant Air Raid Warden. Part of my dad and Norman's responsibility as Air Raid Warden/Assistant Warden was to take a wood-splitting maul and bang it against a railroad rail that was hanging from a tree on the other side of River Road, just across from our house, if the Germans started invading. The maul was pretty heavy, and the rail was pretty high up on the tree. To be safe, my dad thought he and Norman should practice a few times to make sure they did it – or, more to the point, Norman did it – right. After all, the very safety of West Arlington and the entire U.S. depended on it.

Well, try as he could, Norman couldn't swing that thirty-pound maul up and over to hit the rail to save his life. He swung and missed the rail; sometimes he swung and missed the tree entirely, the weight and momentum of the crowbar throwing him off balance. My dad just stood there without saying a word, leaning on the fence, trying hard not to laugh - this was serious business! - until finally he said,

"Norman. You're fired."

And with that, my dad ceremoniously took Norman's Assistant

Air Raid Warden hat off and slowly walked to the barn without looking back, where he hung it quite unceremoniously over one of the cow stanchions.

Fall

Benedict Camp was a cabin in Benedict's Hollow that was owned by (no surprise!) the Benedict family, but supported by those who used it. It was a gathering place for a close-knit group of locals who hunted, a solid structure with little in the way of physical comforts. But, it was a place to sleep and eat, or have barbecues and clambakes, and it was an important place for a group of close friends - husbands and wives - in West Arlington.

Benedict Camp was also a place to play practical jokes. One time while Roger Wilcox was sleeping, Doc Smith reached over and cut off his tie (after he had had a bit of Jack Daniels, I might add). The next night while Doc Smith slept, Roger pulled on the ends of Doc's socks and cut them off, leaving Doc's toes exposed to the cold air. Such pranks were common, and were always in good fun - no one ever got angry, but they *did* usually get even.

Although Norman didn't particularly like to hunt, he loved to go up to Camp. He enjoyed the camaraderie of the folks who were there, and both he and Mary enjoyed the cookouts and socializing that often took place during hunting season. He even donated an original illustration to the camp.

"What do you think?" Norman asked my mother after proudly hanging the illustration on the camp wall.

"Well....you know I love your paintings, Norman, but..." my

mother's voice trailed off. Seeing Norman's distress, she quickly added, "it's just too...too...*nice* for camp. It doesn't really...fit the mood here at camp," she finally explained, gesturing around the room.

"Well, then, I'll get another one!" said Norman, quickly brightening at my mother's explanation.

Soon after, Norman brought the original painting of "Strictly A Sharpshooter" up to camp. Norman had illustrated it a few years before for an issue of *American Magazine* and it had many Arlington locals in it, including Meade Schaeffer's wife, Gene Pelham, Clarence Decker, and Nip Noyes.

"Perfect!" said my mother, smiling, as Norman hung it on the wall over the fireplace.

"Perfect," agreed Norman, walking over to stand by my mother and looking at the painting from across the room.

Years later, Bob Benedict's widow, Betty, sold the illustration for a hefty sum. There were a lot of hard feelings about that, as Norman had given the painting to the people who supported the Camp, not to Bob Benedict personally. The original illustration ultimately made its way to the Norman Rockwell Museum in Stockbridge, where it hangs to this day.

Sunday, November 14th

On Saturday night, I had spent the night up at Benedict Camp. It was the first time I had slept there. At thirteen, I felt pretty grown up to be a part of the overnight hunting group. While my dad had stayed at the farm to do Sunday morning's chores, I was going to go hunting with Doc Smith when we got up. Eddie Killian, head of Draper's Mill in nearby Woodford, had been at camp Saturday night, too. He had shot an eight-point buck on Saturday and was going back out on Sunday to bring in a bobcat that Bob Benedict had shot the day before.

The next morning Eddie got up early and headed out alone. While heading up to Wilson Hollow, he was shocked to see a huge black bear running through the woods, uncommon for Vermont. The bear was only about twenty feet away from him. He shot at it and the bear turned and charged him. Ed kept firing, shooting three more times, and the bear finally collapsed, dead when it was only about ten feet away from him. Turns out that the first shot had been the one to kill the bear, the other three had missed it entirely.

Up on the ridge Sunday morning, my mother had taken Tommy out hunting with her. They heard Eddie's shots and came running, as did Doc Smith and I. We all stood there, shocked, at the sight of the huge bear. Eddie was sitting down on a log, still trying to get his heart back in his chest at the close call he'd just had.

Together with Eddie and Monk Grover, another local hunter, we all pulled the three hundred and twenty pound black bear down to camp. Tommy and I walked back to the farm and that night, the grown-ups held a victory dinner at camp. My dad and Norman had driven up to camp together so that they could join in the fun. The "adult drinks" were flowing as the celebration continued late into the night. My dad had had a bit too much to drink and Norman drove him home and put him to bed. Norman was happy to take my dad home, he loved being around the guys and having fun, and was glad to see my dad let loose a little bit. He also loved to drive my dad's farm truck, and my dad being unable to drive was as good a reason as any!

A few days later, Norman wrote a letter to the editor of the Bennington Banner and sent it along with a photo of the bear, Doc Smith, my mother, Eddie, Tom Green, Tommy, and my dad. In the letter to the editor, Norman tells the story of the bear hunt, finishing with, "Please may I get a job as a reporter? Sincerely, Norman Rockwell. P.S. 'Thar's bar in them thar hills.'"

Saturday, December 25th

In the six months we had lived next door to the Rockwells, we had grown very close, more like family than friends. The differences in our backgrounds didn't mean a thing. There was almost an unwritten code between the families that whatever needed to be done was done, no matter what it was and no matter who had to do it. When the snow had started to fall and the common driveway between us was covered, my father plowed out not only the driveway, but also the driveways that branched off and led up to the Rockwell house and ours. When cash was tight in our house, Norman had lent my dad a small sum of money to buy a pure-bred cow, which my dad promptly repaid as soon as the milk check came in. My dad *always* repaid a debt. When Norman and Mary went out of town, the three boys stayed with us and my folks made sure they were well taken care of. Mary and my mother spent long hours talking. The boys learned about farm living and life in general from my dad when Norman was too busy working, which was most of the time. And me, I was the big brother to the boys they never had, and they were the little brothers to me I had lost.

Christmas morning came and yet another perfect tree from our woodlot stood decorated in the corner. With money being tight, the presents under our tree were mostly functional – new gloves or new boots, a book, a warm sweater. After we had opened everything, we had to do our morning chores like any other day – the cows didn't know it was a holiday. But once the chores were out of the way, we raced over to the Rockwells to see what they had gotten, without any sense of jealousy or envy. We accepted the simple fact that we were poor and they were not, and that they would have more presents than we did.

The four of us kids stomped through the snow and mom and dad followed. Ardis got to the door first and she opened it and walked right in, and all of us went in behind her. Norman was standing in the parlor with his pipe in his mouth watching the boys, and Mary came in from the kitchen. The boys were on the floor still in their pajamas, deep in the middle of a bunch of boxes that said "F.A.O. Schwarz" and wrapping paper like I had never seen before in my life. Everyone shouted "Merry Christmas!" and all of the girls hugged one another. Norman and my dad shook hands firmly, then half hugged, clapping one another on the back the way men do when they're too embarrassed to really give one another a hug. Christmas music blared from the hi-fi and there were beautiful glass ornaments and decorations throughout the whole room.

We had gifts for all of the boys, but I don't honestly remember what they were. Probably something handmade, we didn't have much money for presents. Mary and Norman had something for each of us, too, a new book. Mary had been a schoolteacher and loved to read; she even went into classrooms at school and read to the children on a regular basis. We didn't have many books, and it was wonderful for all of us to have a book of our very own.

After we exchanged gifts, Mary offered Ardis a tin full of candy that the Brown and Bigelow Company, the publisher of the Boy Scout calendars, had sent to Norman. It was the biggest tin of candy any of us had ever seen. Not worrying about being polite, Ardis reached in and took two big handfuls, and Mary just laughed. Seeing that Ardis didn't get in trouble, Edith, Joy, and I all reached in and took two big handfuls, too. I ate some right away, but put the rest in my pocket for later. It was some of the best tasting candy I had ever had – little ribbons of sugar that was so hard, it dissolved on your tongue slowly.

Christmas – like the candy – had never been so sweet.

CHAPTER FIVE
WEST ARLINGTON, VERMONT
1944

Early Spring

The Edgerton and Rockwell houses both had had more than a few difficult winters and the paint on the outside of both houses looked it. I won't say that the Rockwell's house looked shabby yet, but ours sure did.

One morning in early Spring, my dad was on his way down from taking the cows up to pasture and he stopped in for his morning chat with Norman.

"Whatcha workin' on, Norman?" he asked.

"Well," said Norman, "I was sitting here thinking about paint."

"Paint?" asked my dad, "Like, what colors to paint? Or, mixing paint?"

"No," said Norman, "I was thinking about how our houses looked like they needed paint."

My dad took a step over to the window and looked at the back of both houses.

"Can't disagree with you there, Norman," he said, "but I need to wait a bit, seems this time of year, all of my money is going out, not in."

"I understand," Norman said slowly, reaching for his pipe. "But you know, Jim, I was also sitting here thinking about how many times you plowed the driveway out for Mary and me this past winter, and how much we appreciated it when you and Clara took care of the boys before Christmas when we had to go down to New York."

"No problem, Norman, we're neighbors, and that's what neighbors do," said my dad, "we do what we can and we share the responsibility when we're able."

"Well," said Norman, now puffing on his pipe and looking at the canvas in front of him and not at my dad, "I was also thinking about how neighbors share not only responsibility – sometimes, they also share...paint."

And with that, a few weeks later, both the Rockwell and Edgerton houses were shining white on River Road, share and share alike.

Late May

Life on the farm was not easy for my mom or sisters, it was plain, hard work. There were at least seven of us living in the house during my later childhood – my folks, the four kids, and my grandmother, plus hired help from time-to-time – so the cooking, cleaning, laundry, and other house chores kept my mom busy. Like my dad, her day started before the sun came up and lasted until well after it had set. Edith, my older sister, helped Mom a lot; my younger sisters, Joy and Ardis, each had their "jobs" to do, too.

It's hard to imagine that my mom was only twenty years old when her fourth child, Ardis, was born. I guess she always had a strong constitution, whether raising a family, working in the house, or even going deer hunting. She could handle a shotgun or rifle as well as any man, and better than most. Once, she even bagged an eight-point buck on her own, across the river on the bridge lot. Norman was so impressed when he saw it, that he had its head mounted as a gift, a true gesture of his respect for my mom. Mom and Dad thought Norman might like to have it, so they gave it back to him, and he proudly hung that huge deer head right on his studio wall! If you look at just about every photo of Norman in his Arlington studio, you can see his easel set up, right beneath it. That meant a lot to my mother, to have her hunting trophy be a part of Norman's studio. Yes, Mom was truly an amazing woman, and a strong, tough role model for my three sisters.

Like Edith, Joy and Ardis learned a lot from my mother. But, they also learned a lot from Mary Rockwell. Both girls spent a lot of time over at the Rockwell house, and it was obvious Mary enjoyed having them around. Typically, she was surrounded by guys - Norman was usually in the studio, and her three rough and tumble sons constantly ran through the house. In a nice way, my sisters were the daughters Mary never had, and she treated them with kindness and respect. Joy and Ardis came to love Mary as their second mother.

Mary was very different from our mother, and she gave an alternative view of life to my sisters. Where our mom was strong and tough, Mary was more fragile; she was educated and refined. Our house was full of functional handmade furniture and dishes;

Mary's home was filled with antiques, china, and crystal. In the living room, Mary had had a huge bookcase built that almost covered the entire wall, filled with beautiful books of all kinds. Our mom didn't have much time for reading, and books were expensive. Between the two households, the girls learned and enjoyed the best of both worlds.

Even though Mary had live-in household help, she would pay Joy and Ardis to help around their house. It was a way to let my sisters earn some money of their own. It was funny, though. For all her sophistication, Mary was pretty particular about some things, like how the beds were made. To this day, my sisters remember how they were taught the "right way" to change the linens by Mary: Remove the bottom sheet for washing. Take the top sheet and rotate it to the bottom, since the top side of the top sheet was theoretically still clean. By rotating the linens, Mary proudly pointed out to my sisters, she cut the expense of washing the bedding in half.

Many of the Rockwell's friends from New York would summer in Vermont. The friends held a lot of parties, and oftentimes, Mary would arrange for one of my sisters to help. It was another way for the girls to earn a little spending money, and they both enjoyed working at some of the nicer homes in town.

One particular dinner party stands out in Joy's memories of Norman. When Joy was just twelve years old, Mary arranged for Joy to help with a dinner party at the Rockwells' friends, the Woodmans. They normally lived in New Jersey, but like many wealthy people in New York, they had a summer home in Arlington, and the Woodmans wanted to have a big bash to start off the summer's social season. In truth, they also wanted to give their out-of-town friends a chance to rub elbows with their friend, the famous artist, Norman Rockwell.

Don't get me wrong - the Woodmans were nice people. Mrs. Woodman's "claim to fame" was that she had written a fictional story of the Mormons, "Glory Spent," which was published in 1940. Even though she was from Utah, she apparently didn't like the Mormons very much. Mr. Woodman worked for a New York chemical company, American Chemical. He worked long hours, and we later learned – along with Mrs. Woodman – that he had been a part of the Manhattan Project. No one knew that until after the bomb was dropped, and once it was known, we didn't talk about it. Vermonters don't talk about things like that; like I've said before, it's just not the way things are done. At the dinner party, it was all about fun and having a nice time – and, a little bit, showing off Norman.

Joy was excited to go to the Woodman's beautiful home, but a little scared, too, because she had never helped with such a fancy party and she didn't really know what to do. And, at the last minute, Mary was unable to go to the party for Norman, which made Joy even more nervous. She had counted on seeing Mary's familiar face that evening. But, Mrs. Woodman was very kind, and showed her what she needed to do, assuring her she knew that Joy would do a good job.

It took all afternoon to get everything ready for the big event. Evening came, and Joy peeked from the kitchen as the guests began arriving. She thought the ladies looked so beautiful in their party dresses, walking in high heels, their hair and make-up like movie stars. The hors d'oeuvres and drinks were being served in the spacious parlor, just a few feet away from the dining room table that Joy had carefully set with beautiful crystal, china, and sterling silver that she had polished a few hours before. Music was playing, and everyone was laughing, talking – everyone except Norman.

As Joy watched, she noticed that it seemed many of the "summer people" made a beeline for Norman. It seemed odd to the twelve-year old, she didn't understand what the fuss over Norman was all about. She also noticed that Norman didn't seem very relaxed with all of the attention. He didn't say much, just nodded his head, drawing on his pipe. Sometimes Joy noticed that he would look around and not quite pay attention to the person talking right in front of him. He wasn't being rude, he was just – uncomfortable. When Joy replenished the hors d'oeuvre trays or took away the used dishes, Norman would go out of his way to talk to her. Several times in the beginning of the evening, he even came into the kitchen and sat down and chatted with Joy, before Mr. or Mrs. Woodman would come in and kiddingly corral him back out into the parlor.

When it came time to serve the dinner, the guests were summoned to the dining room to sit down. Joy was in the kitchen, getting ready to help carry the first course to the guests. She was alone in the kitchen, when she heard the door open, and Norman quietly walked in. He came to her, smiling, and told her he wanted to say good-bye to her. He was leaving, because he had to take tickets at the Grange Hall for the Saturday night dance. Norman asked her to please tell Mrs. Woodman thank you, but that he had needed to go. He then gave Joy a big smile and a quick hug good-bye before leaving out the kitchen door into the backyard, totally unaware he had been the guest of honor at the party and that he surely would be missed at the dinner table that evening.

When Mrs. Woodman came into the kitchen looking for Norman, Joy dutifully delivered Norman's message. Mrs. Woodman looked startled, flustered, and glanced toward the dining room. Then, she turned toward Joy, let out a deep breath, and quietly said half to herself, "That's Norman."

Saturday, June 3rd

I was always a good athlete and played baseball and basketball on the school's teams all the way through high school, ending up Captain of the basketball team my senior year. Tommy was a pretty good, athlete, too. He was three years younger than I was, but he and I were the closest of the three Rockwell boys. Peter was six years younger than I was, so he was pretty much the tag along kid, and Jerry wasn't much interested in the things I liked to do, like hunting, fishing – and sports.

The Rockwell boys quickly became part of the gang of guys who hung out on a hot summer's evening and often we all trooped over to the Green after dinner to play a game of baseball or just throw around the ball or bat and catch fly balls.

One night we were batting balls and I was in the outfield, about ten feet from Jerry. Tommy, Gordon Clark, and Millard Vaughan were there, too. Peter had followed us over, but when the big kids wouldn't play with him, he got frustrated and walked home without any of us really noticing.

The other guys and I were pretty serious about playing, really into what we were doing, but Jerry was in the outfield goofing around, like always. He walked around and kicked the dirt. At one point he sat down for a while, bored that no balls were coming his way. When they did come close to him, he just sat there or stood there watching as the balls went to his right, left, behind him or in front of him, before pretty casually walking over and picking up the ball to throw it back to somebody. It's not that he wasn't good at throwing, he just didn't care so much about it.

The sun was halfway down when Millard began tossing the baseball in the air as he stood on home base and hitting the ball into the outfield to us. After several hits, Millard hit the ball so hard the bat almost flew out of his hand. It was a beautiful line drive toward the outfield where Jerry was standing, not paying attention, when –WHACK! – it hit Jerry square in the head. I was close enough that I heard a loud *crack* as the ball hit him. Though it knocked Jerry down, unbelievably, it did not knock him out. We all rushed over to him and he got up and just sorta shook his head. I walked him home, and the other guys kept playing a bit as the sun went all the way down, still talking about how Jerry must have a pretty hard head. Now, I know some other writers have said that the ball hit a tree and then hit him in the head, but that's not how it happened. There are no trees on that part of the Green, it's just a wide open field, and, so now you know. Just wanted to set that record straight.

When Jerry got home, his folks knew something was terribly wrong and they took him to the hospital right away. Turned out, his skull was fractured. Millard and Gordon and all the guys felt real bad, so the next day I took up a collection from the guys of about three or four dollars and got him a store-bought fruit basket, and my mom drove me down to the hospital to give it to him. I went into his room and he was joking around and being Jerry. He always had a smile on his face, and he was goofing around with the nurses. I'm not sure he liked the fruit basket itself, but he liked that we had tried to do something nice after Millard beaned him in the head, even if it was an accident. Back in those days, it seemed that giving someone in the hospital a fruit basket could cure anything.

Tuesday, June 6th

School was almost out for the year and I was looking forward to getting eighth grade behind me and getting on to my "real" first year of high school, in the main wing, reserved for ninth to twelfth graders.

I came home and headed over to see if Tommy wanted to go fishing, but he wasn't there. I went out back and headed toward Norman's studio, because a lot of times Tommy was with his dad, watching, or getting a Coke. Norman always put a bunch of ice in the small kitchen sink in the back of the studio and stashed small bottles of Coke in it to keep them cold while he was working, that way he didn't have to take the time to go back into the house. He always let us have one anytime we wanted.

As I started walking to the studio, I almost ran into Norman coming out. He had several pieces of paper in his hands and, as I watched, he walked over to the incinerator and burned them, one at a time. I had seen him do that many times before, as had my dad many mornings when he was taking the cows up the pasture, and we didn't think a thing about it. Little did we know then that Norman was destroying what could later have been sketches of great value

– nowadays, we kiddingly call it the "million-dollar incinerator."

"Have you seen Tommy?" I asked Norman.

Norman shook his head, "Nope, sure haven't Buddy, but I think I saw him head over to your barn a bit ago." With that, I headed home and out to the barn, and Norman walked back into his studio.

Once my eyes got adjusted to the darkness of the barn, I saw my dad and Tommy standing over near the cows' radio. Instead of the normal music, there was news playing, but it didn't sound like the regular farm reports that came on throughout the day, and from the look on my dad and Tommy's faces, I knew it had to be something important. I walked closer over to where they were standing and caught the last of the announcement:

"...as we know more details. Repeating, Allied forces have successfully invaded the beaches at Normandy..."

I immediately thought about Art Becktoft and hoped it would mean he would make it home soon. He had been a real role model to me and was a hero to us all; it had been heartbreaking to hear he had been shot down and captured the year before. As I stood there, I thought back to the fall of 1942, just before he enlisted in the Army Air Corp. I was twelve years old, and I remembered Art coming up the dirt road from the covered bridge with his rifle in his hand. He was tall, handsome, and excited.

"I just shot a six-point buck across the Battenkill," he said, "and I sure would appreciate borrowing your farm truck to get it home." So my dad had stopped working and fired up the truck, and we went down and helped him get his first white-tail buck back to his house. That's how things were in those days. You helped your neighbor, your friend, without thinking about it. You stopped what you were doing to lend a hand. You didn't keep score, it all evened out in the end.

My thoughts came back to the barn. In the excitement of the moment, all thoughts of fishing had gone out of my head, one of the few times that ever happened.

Mid-June

In addition to modeling for "I Will Do My Best," I had earned five dollars when Norman had photographed my cow for "Mrs. O'Leary's Cow," an illustration that was supposed to commemorate the great Chicago fire. In the illustration, a woman – Norman's cook, Elizabeth LaBombard – sat beside my cow, Elsie, milking it while the cow was turned around and looking at her. I had the job of holding Elsie's head to make sure she stood still, and since it was my cow and I was a part of the modeling session, even though I wasn't actually in the illustration, I still got five dollars. The Brown & Bigelow calendar company hadn't liked the idea and neither did Norman, so it was never printed, and if you look at the photo from that day you can see why. No one really wanted to see the big back end of my cow on their calendar.

"One of my biggest flops," he said, laughing at himself, which made it a-ok to laugh with him.

It was a pretty summer day, and Tommy and I had been throwing the baseball in a game of catch just outside Norman's studio. Norman opened the door and called to us, and asked us to come in for a few minutes. Gene Pelham was there, adjusting his camera. Norman wanted Tommy and me to model for him. He showed us what he wanted us to do, then stood back and gave us directions while Gene snapped the pictures. The new modeling job was for another Boy Scouts calendar and I got to wear the same uniform as I had the first time. This time, though, it fit a whole lot better - I had grown quite a lot since the summer before.

In the illustration, I have my hand reached around a Cub Scout, showing him how to tie a knot. Norman had Tommy pose as the Cub Scout. Not only was he the right age, Norman liked to use his family or even himself when he could, to save money, but only if they had the right look for what he wanted to illustrate. He was fair that way, he never cut corners on quality, but he was smart about how he spent his work budget, too.

Tommy was pretty fidgety that day, he was more interested in us going back outdoors and playing than modeling for his dad. But even though Tommy wasn't as cooperative as he should have been, Norman never raised his voice or got angry. He tried to explain carefully what he wanted, and told Tommy he'd give him a toy if he sat still and did as he was told. Immediately, Tommy was the perfect model. Norman wasn't above bribing his own kids if he had to, which on occasion he did.

The session didn't take too long and when we were done, I got my white envelope with five dollars in it. After we changed back into our regular clothes, I ran and put it in my room before heading back out the door and playing catch some more with Tommy. The illustration, "Guiding Hand," featuring two non-Boy Scout models, was published as the 1946 Boy Scout calendar.

Early July

Tommy and I were nuts about baseball. Well, let me rephrase that. *I* was nuts about baseball, especially the Brooklyn Dodgers, and pretty much everything I liked, Tommy liked, too. He was a great kid, and I didn't mind having him around. Usually, I was pretty much a loner or was with older kids, like Stan Deverman or Art Becktoft, but for the first time I had a surrogate little brother and I took the role and the responsibility very seriously.

Norman and Mary encouraged the friendship between us. We never knocked on one another's door, our house was always open to the Rockwell boys and theirs was always open to my sisters and me, we just went on in whenever we wanted. It was like we kids had two houses to live in. If I wanted to listen to the baseball game on a Saturday afternoon, I went in the Rockwell living room and helped myself to their much better radio, whether Tommy was around or not. Tommy hung out with my dad and helped on the farm even when I wasn't there. And, whatever we boys cooked up to do together, Norman said ok. He let me put a basketball hoop up on the side of their barn for us to practice with. He let us camp alone out back in the upper pasture and never thought a thing about his boys being near a roaring campfire with no grown-up around. When Tommy wanted a tennis court for us to play on, Norman had one built behind their house.

I heard Norman and my dad talking about the friendship between the boys and me one time, but it was totally by accident. It was a little after seven o'clock one morning, and my dad had led the cows across our backyard and had walked along the property line between our house and the Rockwell's as he did each morning, headed up to our top pasture. As he was headed back down the hill, like clockwork, Norman was on his way out of their back door, a Coke bottle sticking out of his back pocket, crossing the yard and heading toward the studio.

"Mornin' Norman."

"Mornin' Jim."

"Whatcha workin' on, Norman?" my dad had asked, as he did each day.

"Come on in and see," Norman had said, his reply the same as it was every morning. My dad went into the studio to chat for just a few minutes, to see Norman's latest illustration, and – more likely than not – to comment on it honestly, before Norman started working at his easel and my Dad's chores called him home.

I had needed to ask my dad a question and had walked up to the screen door of the studio, when I heard Norman talking about, of all things, me. He wasn't a man of many words, and neither was my dad, but they had this way of talking between them that was as much what they didn't say as what it was. The bond between them had grown very strong, very fast.

When I think about it now, there couldn't be two more unlikely friends, but that's what my dad and Norman had become. My dad had just a sixth grade education; Norman had attended art schools in Manhattan. My dad had begun working the farm at twelve, same as I had; Norman had grown up in New York City. My dad had never traveled far from West Arlington, Vermont. Norman had traveled the world. Norman hired tree surgeons to come and inspect his trees and then paid to have the dying ones cut down. My dad - who absolutely did not understand what a tree surgeon was or why you would waste your money to pay for one to come to your house – checked his own trees, and took a saw from the barn and cut down any of his trees that needed to be cut.

But, there were similarities, too. Both men had a tremendous work ethic and valued their work. Both men loved their wives and kids, even if my dad spent more time with Mom and us kids than Norman spent with his family. Both men were respectful of people they met, regardless of their circumstances. Both men tried to live a life that reflected the goodness in all of us. I suppose it's fair to say that even though they came from two completely opposing backgrounds, when all was said and done, they ended up sharing the same middle.

"...he's a fine young man and, I tell ya, Jim, as far as I'm concerned, Buddy can do no wrong. In all my years, I've never met such a fine, well-adjusted young man as Buddy."

"Yep, he is," my dad had simply said, in as few words as possible, spoken like a true Vermonter, even though I'm sure he was very proud at that moment.

"He's a fine young man," Norman said again, "a fine young man."

That had made me feel so good, to know Norman had that much trust and confidence in me, although I never let on I had heard him say it. But that day, I did walk around with my head just a little bit higher than usual.

Mid-July

The Brooklyn Dodgers were having a losing season, but I was never a fair weather fan, they were still my team. They'd lost sixteen straight games on the road and I got it in my head that I wanted to see a game for real, that somehow if I were there *personally* cheering them on, their losing streak would be broken. I told Tommy what I was thinking, and he got all excited, too. If we *both* were there, two of the most diehard Brooklyn Dodgers fans ever, winning would be a shoo-in.

We checked the game schedule in the New York Daily News, which was pretty available just over the line in Vermont. The Dodgers were coming home to Ebbets Field on July 18th in a game against the St. Louis Cardinals, then a three-game series against the Cincinnati Reds, followed by a four-game series against the Pittsburgh Pirates. If Tommy and I were going to see them play, that was the timeframe to do it.

A few days after first talking, Tommy and I were walking along the Battenkill, skipping rocks across the water, trying to come up with a plan. We watched as one of my rocks bounced four times, more than halfway across the river, before it sank. The best skip so far.

"I bet my dad would let us go if Jim said it was ok," said Tommy, hopefully, tossing another rock that immediately sank in the water, making a big plopping sound.

"I don't know, Tommy," I said shaking my head, looking around in the tall grass for another good skipping rock, "I've never been to New York before and I'm not sure my folks would let us go by ourselves."

"But, look," he said, turning to me, spreading out his hands as he talked, "if I told my dad that Jim said it was ok, he would say yes; and I bet if you told your dad that *my* dad said it was ok, *he* would say yes. So…I could talk to my dad and you could talk to yours, and…and… and that way they'd both think the *other* dad said ok, and we'd get to go!" he said, proud of his logic, his lisp getting heavier the more excited he got.

"It might work," I said slowly, seeing the sheer genius in his plan. "But if we're gonna do it, we need to do it quick."

We spent the rest of the day down at the swimming hole to get some relief from the July heat. That night, we hiked up behind our houses and put up a lean-to tent, camping out in the cool mountain air. We were still talking about going to see the Dodgers and when we finally had our stories straight and our timing down, we could hardly sleep. Even the mosquitoes didn't bother us too much that night; we were itching more to see the Dodgers in person.

Monday, July 24th

To this day, I don't know how we pulled off going to the Dodgers game, but we had some help. Like many New Yorkers, our neighbor, Bob Smith, lived near New York City during the week and Arlington on the weekends. During the summer months, he would drive his great big Buick down to the City on Sunday night and drive back to Arlington on Thursday night.

I don't know whose idea it was to talk to Bob Smith about taking Tommy and me with him, but regardless, Bob was more than happy to do it. The plan our folks had agreed to was for us to stay with Bob in New Jersey for the nights we were visiting New York, then head back up to West Arlington the end of the week. We left with Bob after dinner on Sunday. On Monday, Tommy and I rode a train into Penn Station and then found our way on the subway to Flatbush and out to Ebbets Field to catch the Dodgers-Pirates game.

After years of laying on the floor for hours and hours listening to the baseball games on the radio, I couldn't believe I was actually sitting in the stands at Ebbets Field. There weren't a lot of people there, the war and a losing record had kept the crowds away, but it didn't matter to Tommy and me at all. We ate hot dogs and popcorn and candy and drank sodas until there wasn't room for even one bite more. We cheered for Bob "Mr. Chips" Chipman, power hitter Dixie Walker, and switch hitter Augie Galan play against Babe Dahlgren and Vince DiMaggio. The Pirates had beat the Dodgers in both games of their double header the day before, but this day was ours. It had to be. I had come all the way from Vermont to see them play, and I wasn't about to see them lose.

As it turns out, the Dodgers did win, twelve to seven. After the game, I guided Tommy back onto the subway and we headed for Manhattan to see our neighbor, Woody Woodman, who worked in New York during the week, too, at the Empire State Building. We got off the subway way too early and ended up walking along the docks in Brooklyn, trying to figure out where we were. It was a pretty tough area, but no one bothered us. Tommy had a matchbox collection, and I can still see him bending over and stooping to pick up filthy dirty matchbox covers discarded by the dock workers. Some of the names and sketches on the matchboxes were "interesting" to see. Ultimately, we got back on the subway at another stop and made our way into the city, and then somehow found our way to the Empire State Building. We just kept walking and asking people for help, and before we knew it, we were standing in front of the Security Desk at 350 Fifth Avenue.

"We'd like to see Mr. Woody Woodman," I said, trying to sound mature.

"Do you know where he works?" asked the young security guard, looking at Tommy and me pretty suspiciously.

"He works at American Chemical Company," I said confidently, pulling Tommy closer to me and putting my arm protectively around his shoulders.

"Yeah, he works for American Chemical Company," Tommy lisped.

The guard eyed us for a minute, then said, "Sixteenth floor, elevators are behind you, on the right."

Tommy and I walked over and hit the elevator button marked "up" and waited for the doors to open. We climbed on the elevator, and I reached up to hit the button marked "sixteen." We zoomed up so fast it made my stomach feel weird, it was the first time I had ever been in such a tall building. When the door opened, it made a funny chiming sound, and we walked out and into a long hallway. At the end of the hallway stood a huge glass double door framed in deep, dark wood that said, "American Chemical Company." I walked in front of Tommy and pushed on the heavy door and it creaked open. After Tommy came in the door, I let go, and I couldn't help noticing that it didn't even bang shut, it slowly and gently closed with a quiet thud all by itself.

In front of us stood a high wooden counter, and an older woman with big dark-rimmed glasses and bright red lipstick sat behind it, her hair all piled up on top of her head.

"May I help you?" she asked in a bored and heavy New York accent, looking down at us.

"We're here to see Woody," I said, clearing my throat that had suddenly gone dry.

"Woody," she said flatly.

"Yeth, Woody," said Tommy, lisping excitedly. "He'th ecth-pecting uth."

"And, uh, *whom* shall I say is here to see him?" she sarcastically asked, glaring at us.

"Buddy and Tommy," I said simply and as forcefully as I could, glaring at her.

"One moment," she said, looking at me like we were bothering her.

Just then two young men walked through the lobby laughing, but they stopped short when they saw Tommy and me standing there. All of a sudden I was very aware that our clothes were pretty dirty from being at the game, on the subway, and walking around the docks. I'm sure we didn't smell real good, either.

"Mr. Woodman," the woman's voice was all one tone into the phone handset, "a 'Buddy and Tommy' are here to see you?"

I watched her face go from insulting to worried all in a few seconds.

"Yes, sir, I will do that," she said nicely, suddenly smiling and nodding her head up and down as she looked at us, "I understand. Ok, I will. Yes, yes, I will. Ok, I understand. Yes, sir. I will, sir. Thank you, sir."

And with that, she smiled a big, fake smile at us and said,

"Would you boys like to have a cold soda? Do you need to go to the men's room? I have some small candy bars here in my desk, are you hungry?"

Before we could say anything, Woody came out from a hallway behind the receptionist's desk and put his arms around each of us, cheerfully walking us back to his office, where there was a plaque on the door that said "President." Tommy looked over his shoulder at the receptionist and smiled a big, fake smile right back at her.

The next few days were a whirlwind. Each morning, we rode on the train into the city, and then Tommy and I went exploring. We would meet Bob or Woody for lunch and then head back out on the streets again in the afternoon. At the end of the day, we met up with Bob for the train ride home to New Jersey for the night. On Wednesday, we ate lunch at a fancy restaurant, and then we saw the Rockettes at Radio City Music Hall.

"WOW!" said Tommy, his eyes wide at the high-kicking gals, "they're THLICK CHICKTHS!"

By the time we rode Jersey Wednesday night, we were pretty beat. Thursday afternoon, we headed back home to Vermont. I had a long time to think about our adventure as we drove. Tommy sat in the seat next to me, reading some comic books Woody had bought us as I looked out the window. Every moment of the trip had been exciting. Unlike Tommy, for me it was a new experience, like going to a foreign country for the first time. I can't say that I would ever want to live in a city like that, but I had handled myself and had taken care of Tommy in a totally unknown situation, and I felt like I had really accomplished something. The fact that we had helped the Dodgers win was pure icing on the cake.

Early August

Norman was asked by Ben Hibbs, his editor at the Post, to illustrate a story that Carl Sandburg had written to commemorate Abraham Lincoln's birthday in February. Norman had a hard time thinking up what he wanted to do, but finally decided on a portrait that I think is one of the finest illustrations he ever did, or that was done by any American artist. I'm no art critic, but I think the majesty of the painting and its symbolism is genius and grace combined.

The illustration shows Abraham Lincoln in the upper left corner looking down at a hurt soldier who sits in the middle of the painting. The people standing and sitting around the soldier are all symbols of freedom, liberty, and democracy in our country. There are old people and young people; immigrants and laborers; a dog tag and military helmet hang on a cross to show respect for those killed in the war; a man holds a blueprint and T-square, showing the rebuilding of the future. In all, eighteen Arlington models appear in the illustration, more than any other painting Norman did while in Arlington.

Walt Squires was the model for an injured soldier. Local farmer Curnel Vaughn is in the illustration holding the blueprints, as is Rose Hoyt, holding her son Gene, the baby she had been pregnant with when Norman had used her in Freedom of Worship the year before. Pat and Lee Schaeffer, Mead's girls, are in it, as is Walt's wife, and local farmer Harold Bridges. The woman on the lower left with the braids is also Rose Hoyt.

For an illustration as special as this, Norman also included the special people in his life. All of the Rockwell boys – Jerry, Tommy, and Peter – are there. And three generations of my family are included, too. That's my grandmother Elva in the upper right side, praying, and my sister, Ardis just below her. My dad is reaching down on the left side of the soldier, holding out his hand. On the lower left corner, my sister Joy joins me and the Rockwell boys. Norman even put himself in, just over my dad's shoulder, looking down at the soldier thoughtfully.

The modeling session for The Long Shadow of Lincoln was different than the other illustrations I modeled for, before or after. First of all, it took longer than most. Second, Norman seemed especially intense when he posed us this time, quieter than usual, and he had our family pose in all different combinations – Joy, Ardis, and I posed separately, but then Norman had Gene take pictures of some of us with Dad or Grandma, and then he'd switch us all around again.

As he worked on the illustration, Norman asked my mom and dad to come and take a look several times. He valued their honest opinions, and they felt comfortable enough with Norman to volunteer their true thoughts. It had become a part of the daily chats between him and my dad to comment on whatever Norman was painting, and many times Norman would call my mother over to the studio as she hung the laundry and ask her opinion, too.

Perhaps it was that respect for one another that made Norman ask my mom and dad to come over for a photo shoot for the two-page center photo in a book that Arthur Guptill was writing entitled, "Norman Rockwell Illustrator." I'll never forget - Norman had asked them to come over at the last minute, and my mom had gotten a little flustered. Even though she didn't say anything, she ran upstairs real quick and changed into a fresh dress and brushed her hair back – not a part of her normal middle-of-the-day routine on the farm, but she would never say no to Norman. He had told them that he wanted to include a photo for the book that showed his family and closest friends looking on, offering their opinions, because that's how he really always worked. And with the photo shoot, as with everything Norman painted, he wanted it exactly as it truly was – other than my mom looking a little more dressed up than she usually was when she came over to the studio to see what Norman was up to, which was just fine with Norman.

Friday, September 15th

For the third time in less than ten years, we were hit again with severe weather. The Great Atlantic Hurricane of 1944 blew through New England bringing high winds and lots of rain. It had been a strong hurricane with winds of more than one hundred fifty miles per hour when it hit Virginia, then it headed north, coming straight across the southern tip of Massachusetts and up through Maine. School was canceled that day and it was useless to do anything else but stay inside. By Saturday afternoon, the sun was out, and "storm clean-up" started to seem like a regular part of our chores.

October

The war was winding down and the news was good. Paris had been liberated in August and the march was on throughout Europe. The war in the Pacific was in full swing and reports came in of raids over Okinawa. It seemed every time we turned the radio on, there was news about a major land invasion or victory. Some of the troops had rotated home, and everyone was hoping the war would soon come to an end.

It may sound odd with how folks think about war now, but the war back then had brought our community together in many ways, young and old. We kids went to the fields and gathered bagfuls of milkweed pods to be used for life preservers and parachutes for the soldiers in the Navy and Army Air Corps. FDR had created the War Production Board in 1942, to ration the use of gas, heating oil, metal, rubber, and plastic that were needed in large quantities during the war. Scrap metal drives were organized under its guidelines and they were a regular community occurrence. At school, we held competitions between classes to see who could gather the most. Each class would weigh what the students had collected and then all of the scrap was put in a huge pile in front of the school, a mountain of metal to help the war effort.

Norman and Mary did their part for the war effort like everyone else, they didn't hold themselves above the community in any way whatsoever. During one of the school scrap metal drives when I was in seventh grade, even though Mary had three boys of her own in school, she gave me a perfectly good aluminum pan when I came to their door looking for donations. When the high school held an auction to raise money and sell war bonds and stamps, Norman gave me a table tennis set to add to the auction, and it sold for five dollars' worth of defense stamps. Members of the War Production Board came to the West Arlington Grange Hall and provided entertainment with a message, a pep talk about increasing agricultural production and civil defense. No doubt Norman's presence and connection to the war effort brought them out to the Valley.

The Rockwells had an eight-passenger station wagon at the time, and Mary took a carload of volunteers on a regular basis over to Troy, New York, to donate blood. One January, my dad plowed high drifts of snow in twenty-five degrees below zero weather so that even in the height of bad weather, Mary could make her blood drive run to Troy.

Norman created many illustrations to help the war effort. Doing what Norman did best, he captured the emotions we felt through the years of fighting: The experiences of our soldiers, shown through Willie Gillis' eyes; the contributions of women to the effort captured in Rosie the Riveter, modeled by Arlington telephone operator Mary Doyle, and Liberty Girl, which showed a woman in stars and stripes holding items that symbolized thirty-one jobs held by women during the war; and the joy that was felt when our soldiers came home, shown in five Post covers published in 1945, including his famous Homecoming GI and Homecoming Marine.

The first illustration Norman painted about our boys coming home was Homecoming GI. He decided to make the soldier come home to a working class family in an urban setting. Since the Arlington area was rural, Norman rode over to Troy and found a spot near the railroad tracks that suited what he needed perfectly. When it came time to pick the models, he called over the fence to my mother and asked her if my ten-year old sister Ardis would help out. Mom said yes, of course, and she called Ardis inside and immediately sent her upstairs to wash her face and comb her hair and to put on her best Sunday dress and shoes, then shooed her out the door and over to the studio.

Ardis proudly walked into the studio for her first of several modeling jobs for Norman.

"Ta-da! I'm here!" she announced loudly to Norman, who had his back to the door. He turned around and his eyes got real big when he saw her.

"Ardis! Don't you look pretty!" he said, smiling at her.

"Yes, Norman, I do," she said nodding, with ten-year old honesty.

"But, uh, how about if you run home and put back on that nice flowered dress you had on when I saw you playing out in the yard earlier today, and maybe leave the hair bow at home?" Norman said gently.

"But Norman," Ardis said very matter-of-factly, "that dress was all dirty and raggedy from digging in the garden."

"Precisely," said Norman, and with that she ran home and changed back into her play clothes.

Homecoming GI was selected by the U.S. Treasury to be the official poster for its latest war bond drive, and more than three hundred thousand copies of it were made and distributed around the country. We Edgertons were proud that Ardis was part of something so important for the war effort. I was also proud of my dog, Spot, because she's in the illustration, too. Spot was my four-year old hunting dog, and Norman paid me five dollars to let her model.

Homecoming Marine was the third of Norman's homecoming covers that were published in 1945. It shows four men and two boys sitting around a Marine in uniform in a mechanic's dark and greasy garage. The young man's face appears on what seems to be the front page of a newspaper article nailed on the wall behind them.

When Norman had to decide how and where to stage the models for this illustration, he called Bob Benedict up at Benedict's

Garage. Like everyone in Arlington, Bob was more than happy to do whatever he could for the likeable Norman. They agreed that Norman and Gene Pelham would come over in a few days to stage and photograph the scene. For the next few days and nights, Bob and his brothers Art and John went to work like madmen, cleaning up the garage. They swept and cleaned the floors and cleared off the stuff on the tables, trying to polish things so that the garage would look good for Norman.

When Norman arrived at Benedict's Garage the next day, he couldn't believe his eyes. Instead of looking like the messy garage he knew, it looked clean and neat. As he quietly looked around, Art, Bob, and John stood by, proud of their hard work. Jerry and Peter were running around the cleared out spaces, arms spread out in the air like war planes, making bombing noises, getting ready to pretend they were talking to a real live soldier.

"Looks pretty…spiffy," Norman said slowly, drawing on his pipe, as he continued to look around the garage, Gene silently next to him.

"Yep," said Bob, "We worked real hard to make it look good for you, Norman."

"You know," said Norman slowly, pointing to a heap in the corner, "it might not hurt to put a few of those rags around a bit, sort of make it look like you were working when the soldier came in."

"Sure, ok," said Art, still feeling proud of what a good job they had done to clean up their garage for the important Post cover.

"And you know," continued Norman slowly, looking over at a pile of tools neatly stacked in another corner, "it might not hurt if you put some of those tools over on the workbench, or scattered them around on the floor, like you had just finished doing something and got interrupted by our soldier coming in and telling his story."

"Sure, ok, no problem," said John, starting to understand what Norman wasn't saying as much as what he was. And so, in Norman's quiet way, without hurting the Benedict brothers' feelings, Norman made sure that the real life of the garage was captured for the Post cover that was published on October 13, 1945.

The powerful illustration shows the inside of a greasy, dark garage. In addition to Jerry and Peter, the back of Herb Squires is on the lower right. Nip Noyes, our Arlington postman and frequent model for Norman, sits in his actual postman's uniform to the right. Bob and John are the two other men in the scene, wearing their normal grease monkey clothes. The young soldier is Duane Parks who sits on a crate holding a Japanese flag, referring to the bitter fight at Iwo Jima. Norman had seen Duane at one of our Grange dances the summer before and when he was considering who to use as the young soldier, he knew Duane would be perfect. Duane wasn't from Arlington, but Art had said he was a fine young man.

The illustration touched the hearts of people in our country deeply. It captured how we all felt about the sacrifice of so many soldiers at Iwo Jima, both proud and somber at the same time.

In May of 2006, it was still touching our hearts. The original oil painting was sold at Sotheby's for $9.2 million.

November

November had arrived and for most males (and some mothers) in Vermont, that meant only one thing – deer season had arrived!

Deer hunting in rural Vermont was sacred, an important part of our culture and our heritage. It wasn't just about the sport of hunting, for our family it was also about the venison that would come from the deer that were shot during the season. We usually ate the deer meat as soon as we butchered it, my mother could cook venison in a lot of ways, even from tough old bucks. My dad had a big storage crock and he would cure all kinds of meat – pork, beef, and venison when we had it – creating a kind of jerky that would last through the winter months, too.

The days leading up to opening day of the season were filled with getting chores out of the way; observing, scouting, and planning where to hunt; and preparing what weapon you were going to use. Even at an early age, I developed a "plan, do, review" approach, including what clothes I needed to start getting together for deer season, making sure my rifle was ready, and other important details.

Opening day of deer season was an unofficial day off from school in rural Vermont. It wasn't written "on the books," so to speak, but it would have been pointless for any teachers to punish any of us for not showing up, as deer hunting on opening day of the season was a given. Even shops were closed, and signs hung in store windows all over town that simply said, "Gone Hunting."

Our daily routine on the farm changed during those weeks, too. We got up two hours earlier, at 3:30 a.m., and had our chores finished by 5:30 a.m., the milk ready and waiting for the 7:00 a.m. pick-up by the milk truck. I headed out the door to hunt around 6:45 at daybreak, and sometimes my dad joined me after the milk was safely on its way. If he went out on his own, he had to return to the barn around 11:00 a.m. to clean the stables, feed the cows, etc., but I – literally – stayed out from sun up to sundown, one of the few times of year I had time off from the daily farm routine.

I preferred to hunt alone. There was something almost magical about being by yourself outdoors in the quiet of the woods, walking softly so you didn't startle the animals, listening with your ears as well as your gut. You had to use all of your senses when you hunted, it made you have to be sharp, noticing changes in the foliage where deer had eaten the lower branches, or seeing their tracks between the fallen leaves in the dirt. Although I had always been a good shot with squirrels, partridge, and small animals, I had never shot a buck. This year, I was hopeful that my time had come.

At the end of the first day of the season, I was up on the ridge behind our house, when all of a sudden I saw a flash of white up a ways in front of me. I moved around a big maple tree quietly and looked up in the direction of the flash, slowly scanning the trees, afraid that my pounding heart was making too much noise and would scare the deer I thought I had spotted away. Nothing. I kept creeping along, slowly moving aside small tree branches clawing at my face, climbing over dead trees, carefully putting one foot in front of the other. I tried to avoid stepping on small twigs that might snap and make a loud noise in the quiet. Nothing. For twenty minutes I continued to inch forward and for twenty minutes – still nothing. I had begun to wonder if my mind had been playing tricks on me, when all of a sudden I heard the familiar sound of heavy movement running through a thick patch of trees to my right. I turned toward the direction of the sound and saw a six-point buck – a legal deer - running in a zig-zag pattern away from me.

My heart was pounding, but my total focus was on that buck. I had a 25-20 rifle, a small caliber pump with a seven-cartridge magazine. I shouldered my rifle and took careful aim, then squeezed the trigger, pumped, and squeezed again six more times, emptying the magazine, but the buck didn't stop. I took off running as I loaded more shells into the magazine. Remembering what my dad had taught me, I ran at a diagonal angle through the brush, flanked the deer, cut it off, and shot again. This time, it went down.

Down below, my dad was in the back field, and he heard the familiar sounds of my rifle. A few minutes later, I was at the edge of the woods, struggling to drag the deer down to the backyard. Jerry and Tommy were in their backyard.

"Boys!" my dad yelled over to them, pointing, "Go help Buddy bring in the buck!"

Jerry and Tommy ran as fast as they could to help me. They would never dream of not doing what my dad said. Between the three of us, we managed to haul my first buck down toward the house. As we got closer, our voices were pretty loud, and my mom and sisters came outside to see what all the commotion was about. My mom was smiling and congratulating me, as my sisters asked a lot of questions about what had happened. Norman poked his head out of the studio door to see what all the ruckus was about and walked over to where we all stood. Jerry, Tommy, and I all were talking over one another as the story of how I shot my first deer grew bigger and bigger.

As everyone stood around congratulating me, chatting and laughing, my dad continued to work in the field. He never looked up, he just kept working, smiling, but saying nothing at all.

West Arlington, the Green (1934) – Clockwise: Edith (6), me (4), Joy, (3) and our baby sister Ardis (approximately 6 months). Behind us, the one-room schoolhouse which burned down in 1936.

West Arlington, the Green (1938) – Schoolchildren file into the new schoolhouse on the left. The Methodist Church (built in 1804) is to the right. In the background, our house sits on the left, the Rockwell's house is on the right.

West Arlington (1936) – At 6, my biggest catch was a 19" rainbow trout, directly from the waters of the Battenkill River.

West Arlington (1940) – At ten, I was already driving the Doodlebug, our homemade tractor. In this photo, I was giving my friend John Bentley a ride.

West Arlington (1940) – Art Becktoft took this shot of my puppy "Spot" and me at the entry of our cellar.

West Arlington, (1943) – Enjoying one of our annual Clam Bakes.

Top photo: Norman and Mary.

Bottom photo: Our family and the Rockwells with friends. Tommy Rockwell (age 10) is lying on the ground. In the front row, my Uncle Bob is far left; my sister Joy is fifth from the left. In the back row, from left to right is my sister Ardis, my dad Jim, Norman, Mary, my mother Clara, my Aunt Amy Stroffeleno, and on the far right, my sister Edith.

West Arlington (1944) – Sugaring has always been an important part of life in Vermont. Mead Schaeffer had my mom and dad pose for this photo, which was a Saturday Evening Post cover on February 17, 1945. My dog Shep is in the foreground and our horses Dick and Prince are patiently hitched to the maple sap gathering sled.

West Arlington (1965) – Three generations of Edgertons sugaring on our farm. From left to right: Me, with a heavy backpack drill; my son, Jim, with his brand new compact drill; and my dad with a good old hand auger.

West Arlington (1944) – Our horse "Dick" pulling our two-person sleigh loaded with five of us! Clockwise: My father Jim, me, and Norman's three sons Tommy, Jarvis, and Peter. Our church and the Grange Hall are in the background.

New Jersey (1944) – Tommy and I had a blast at an amusement park.

West Arlington (1944) – I took this photo in our field during haying season. In front: Billy Brown (a neighbor and Rockwell model). First row from left: My sister Ardis; Al Clary; my mother in the driver's seat of the Doodlebug; Art Becktoft, Jr.; Marilyn Johnson; and my sister Joy. Overseeing it all from the top of haystack, my father Jim.

West Arlington (1944) – Norman was not the only artist who thought our family made great models. Mom and Dad posed for Gene Pelham for a Christmas card painting in our one-horse open sleigh.

West Arlington, Norman's studio (1946) – Norman is holding his dog Butch for a modeling shot which he later used in *Going and Coming*.

West Arlington, Norman's studio (1945) – This picture was taken for Arthur Guptill's book "Norman Rockwell; Illustrator," the first book written about Norman and his art (published 1946). Left to right: Albert Labombard (the Rockwell's handyman), Mary, Elizabeth Labombard (the Rockwell's cook), Peter, my mom and dad, and Norman.

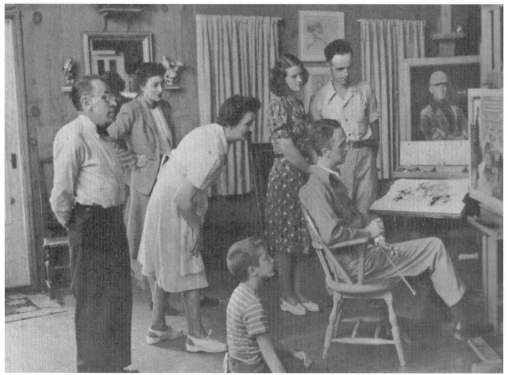

West Arlington (1946) – My mother shot this eight-point buck.
The head hung in Norman's Arlington studio until the Rockwells moved to Stockbridge.

127

West Arlington, Norman's studio (1946) – On October 16th, the sixth grade class of Burlington's Taft School visited Norman at his studio. A student, Alison Pooley, died less than a year later, leading Norman to donate *The Babysitter* original illustration to the class. Upper left: Mary Rockwell's handwritten letter to the class's teacher. Upper right: Norman and Mary greet the students. Bottom: The sixth grade class. (Photos courtesy of Lynn Swan).

129

Stockbridge, Norman's studio (1959) – Norman working on *The Vet*, which he illustrated for the Upjohn Pharmaceutical Company. For my modeling stint as the vet, Norman paid me $50.00. A big pay raise from the $5.00 modeling fee in West Arlington!

West Arlington, our front yard (1961) – Mary died unexpectedly in 1959 at the age of 51. Norman met Mollie Punderson in 1960 in Stockbridge. In the Spring of 1961, he brought Mollie to meet my parents. Norman and Mollie married on October 25, 1961.

Stockbridge, Norman's home (1972) – My folks took a trip to visit Norman and Mollie. Bottom left: Norman and my mother, Clara. Bottom right: Norman and my father, Jim.

Stockbridge, Norman's home (1974) – I went with my parents to see Norman, not knowing it would be my last time to see him before he passed away. Clockwise from left to right: Norman and I pose in front of several of Norman's illustrations; Norman autographs a print of *County Agent* for me as Mollie looks on; saying good-bye to Norman as he took one of his frequent bike rides; my dad, Jim, Norman, and I.

Stockbridge, Norman Rockwell Museum (1993) – The Rockwell boys and I enjoyed being together again to celebrate the opening of the new Norman Rockwell Museum after it moved from its previous location, the Old Corner House. In this photo: Tommy, me, Peter, and Jerry.

Stockbridge, Norman Rockwell Museum (1998) – Dot and I presented the preview of *A Guiding Hand* to Laurie Norton Moffatt, Museum Director.

My first time to pose for
Norman was the illustration,
I Will Do My Best,
a Boy Scout calendar.

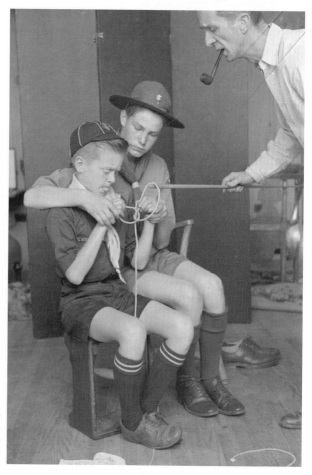

Norman actively participated
in the modeling photos. Here,
he helps create the image of a
perfect knot with Tommy and
me for *A Guiding Hand*.

134

I Will Do My Best
Original oil painting for Boy Scout poster-calendar (1945).

A Guiding Hand
Original oil painting
for Boy Scout poster-
calendar (1946).

My Sister Ardis praying for
The Long Shadow of Lincoln.

My sister Joy pondering for *The Long Shadow of Lincoln.*

In my best Sunday
clothes posing for
*The Long Shadow
of Lincoln.*

My father Jim lending a hand for
The Long Shadow of Lincoln.

Grandma Edgerton kneeling for *The Long Shadow of Lincoln.*

The Long Shadow of Lincoln
Saturday Evening Post inside feature to commemorate Lincoln's birthday (1945).
The title was: "Thoughts on Peace on Lincoln's Birthday" with a subtitle "A Litany by Carl Sandburg."

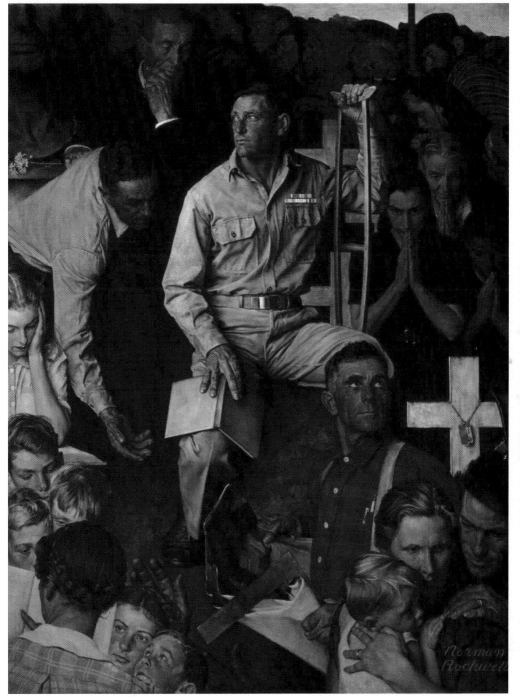

Duane Parks and Peter Rockwell in Benedict's
Garage for *Homecoming Marine*.

Art Becktoft posing for *Back to Civies*.

Norman demonstrating a pose for
Breaking Home Ties.

My last modeling job at Norman's West Arlington
studio for *United Nations*. Unhappy with the
illustration, Norman changed the idea and it became
Golden Rule, commonly called *Do Unto Others*.

Back to Civies
Cover for *The Saturday Evening Post*
by Norman Rockwell (1945).

Homecoming Marine
Cover for *The Saturday Evening Post* by Norman Rockwell (1945).

Golden Rule
Cover for *The Saturday Evening Post*
by Norman Rockwell (1961).

Breaking Home Ties
Cover for *The Saturday Evening Post* by Norman Rockwell (1954).

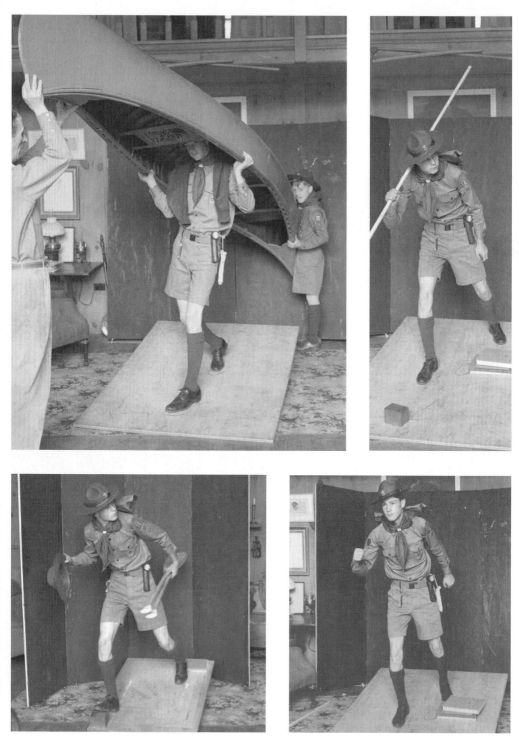

All four pictures above: Modeling for *Men of Tomorrow* was my most work-intensive job for Norman.
I modeled for all of the poses in the painting except Peter Rockwell, who is in the Cub Scout uniform.

norman rockwell

141

Perfectly cast, Norman didn't have to do anything to get Grandma Edgerton's look for his famous *Going and Coming*. She pretty much wore this blank expression all day, but she was a lovely and caring woman.

This photo was shot in front of Norman's garage with John Benedict's car, which he used to deliver mail. The driver is John Cross, the boy out the window is Billy Brown, the woman is Gladys Cross.

Going and Coming
Cover for *The Saturday Evening Post* by Norman Rockwell (1947).

My sister Ardis posing for *The Babysitter*. The baby was Gene Pelham's daughter Melinda (now Murphy). Norman ended up using Lucille Towne for the final painting.

Norman was never shy when it came to showing his models which expressions he wanted for his paintings, here posing with my sister Ardis for what later became a part of *The Dugout*.

Babysitter with Screaming Infant
Cover for *The Saturday Evening Post*
by Norman Rockwell (1947).

The Dugout
Cover for *The Saturday Evening Post*
by Norman Rockwell (1948).

145

Jon's parents, my Uncle Bob (92) and Aunt Amy (88) Stroffoleno, in front of their West Arlington house which they built with their own hands in 1939 and have lived in ever since.

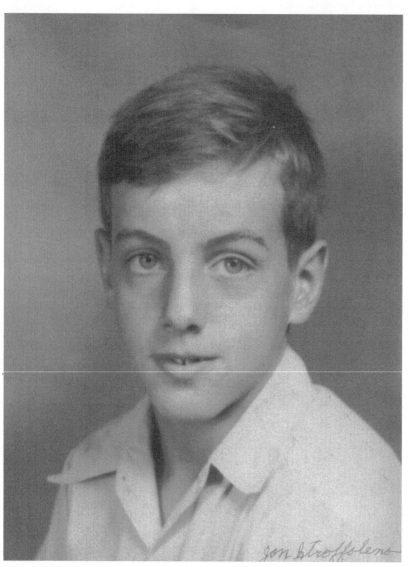

My cousin Jon Stroffoleno's fifth grade school picture.

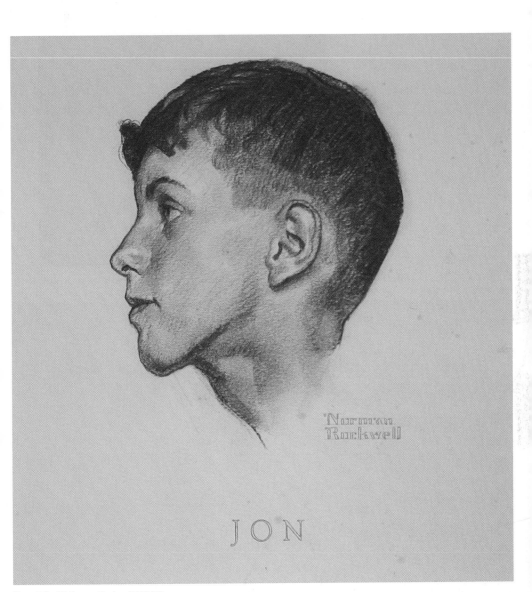

Jon - The Unknown Rockwell (1952)
The previously unknown Rockwell charcoal portrait of Uncle Bob and Aunt Amy's son, Jon. Created from memory for them upon Jon's accidental death, it was a gift from Norman to the family.

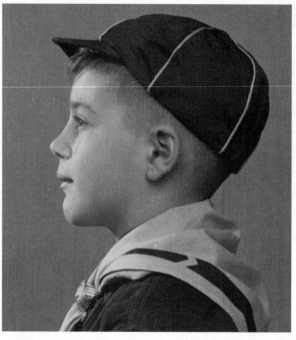

My son James "Jimmy" Edgerton modeling for the Cub Scout in *Growth Of A Leader* at the age of nine.

My modeling shot for *Growth Of A Leader* when I was 34 years old, used for the Scout Leader. Norman aged me ten years for the Scout Master and took off twenty years for the Boy Scout.

148

Growth Of A Leader
Original oil painting for Boy Scout poster-calendar (1966).

Dear Bud,~

At last I have finished
the Boy Scout Calendar that you
and your noble son posed for
down here in Stockbridge, last year.

Brown and Bigelow
insist on these releases or I
don't get paid. It, the picture,
turned out quite well.

Give my very, very best
to your family and Clara and
Jim. Enclosed is five bucks to
pay the notary.

Best wishes and thanks

Cordially

Norman

Letter from Norman after I modeled for *Growth Of A Leader*.

CHAPTER SIX
WEST ARLINGTON, VERMONT
1945 - 1947

1945

January

The winter started out brutal. It had been snowing almost continuously for weeks. For chores, this kind of weather made everything more difficult. For fun, well, that was something else.

Back up behind our two houses there was a big pond. The water in the pond was frozen over hard enough that we could skate and slide on it. We called it the "Edgewell Pond," Edgerton and Rockwell put together, and for hours and hours each winter, the seven of us kids played together on our own personal outdoor skating rink. Sometimes my folks and Mary came out and joined us, chasing us around. A couple of times, we even convinced Norman to come out of the studio and spend some time with us on the ice. Unlike my dad, he wasn't very coordinated, but he really tried.

"Norman," said Ardis, sliding and falling down next to him on purpose, where he had fallen, laughing, "I think your painting is better than your ice skating."

"Can't argue that, Ardis," he said, still laughing and shaking his head as he tried to stand before slipping on the ice again, "can't argue that."

Late April

As soon as there was any hint of warm weather, Tommy and I headed outside to play catch. It had been a hard winter, and we couldn't wait to get outside to throw the ball around.

One Saturday afternoon in April, we played catch on the grass right in front of Norman's studio. It was the perfect spot, a wide open area with nothing in the way of throwing the ball around. Sometimes while we were tossing the ball back and forth, I saw Norman standing at the big, plate glass window, his pipe in his mouth, looking out and watching us.

"Hey Buddy!" called Tommy as he ran backwards a ways, "throw it over here!"

I raised my arm behind my head in a pitcher's stance. I was a pitcher on the high school baseball team and this was a good chance to practice my throwing arm. As I extended my arm forward and released the ball in what was intended to be a chest high, easy-to-catch ball for Tommy to handle, the ball flew high off my fingers and rose high into the air – and right through the center of Norman's large studio window.

I just stood there, too scared to move, as pieces of glass fell out of the window and onto the ground. Tommy ran up and stood beside me.

"Wow!" he said, "I think you threw it all the way to the top of the stairs!"

A few minutes later we were still standing there, frozen with fear, when the door opened and out came Norman, holding our ball in his hand.

"You might want to move a bit over that way," he said to us, pointing away from the studio toward the back of their house. Then, he tossed the ball underhand to Tommy and turned to go back inside the studio, raising his hand in the air in a kind of wave before I could even apologize.

That was it. No yelling, he didn't seem angry, nothing. Tommy and I looked at each other and Tommy shrugged.

"Let's go," he said, tossing the ball up in the air as he walked over toward the house.

That night at dinner when I told my folks what had happened, my parents looked at each other a little worried. Replacing the window was going to be expensive and money was always an issue in our house. But when my dad tried to speak to Norman about it the next day, Norman just shook his head and laughed.

"No problem, Jim," he had said, "they're boys, they're good boys, it happens."

The next morning, Walt Squires replaced the glass and, true to his word, there was no discussion about my paying for it. At the end of the day, I had a few minutes between chores and supper. Tommy was out back and I went over next to him, to check out the new window. It looked great. You couldn't even tell it had been replaced.

"Did he ever say anything?" I asked Tommy quietly as I looked through the window and saw Norman sitting there, working.

"Nope," he said, shaking his head, looking through the window at his dad, too, "not a word."

I felt as if a giant weight had been lifted off my shoulders. I had really been concerned that Norman was mad at me, let alone worrying about how I was going to pay for the broken window. But, it seemed everything was forgiven and all was ok. I relaxed for the first time since my fatal throw the day before.

With a little bit of time before I had to go inside to eat, Tommy and I decided to hit a few fly balls. Tommy was batting and I easily caught the first three pop-ups. The fourth time, Tommy threw the ball up into the air and hit it again, but the toss wasn't that good and the swing wasn't much better. The ball sailed too high over my head for me to catch it. I quickly ran backwards, keeping my eye on the ball, but it was beyond my reach. I stood and watched helplessly as the ball started to arc down, down, down – right through the newly replaced studio window.

It was as if my feet were planted in the ground and I was a stone statue. I couldn't move, I couldn't talk, I just stood there, staring, not believing what I had just seen, what had just happened. Tommy stood there, frozen too, looking at the big, jagged pieces of glass still stuck in the window.

Norman came out of the studio door. Looking up at the broken window, he quietly said, "Well, boys, guess I'll go call Walt," then he turned and walked back inside the studio.

That's just the way he was.

Monday, May 7th

The war in Europe was over! The Germans had surrendered. When we heard the news, everyone in town was yelling and celebrating, blowing their car horns, banging on pots, and dancing around. We had beat the Germans, and our boys were coming home!

I went over to the Rockwells and listened to the radio with Tommy, Jerry, and Mary. Even Peter sat along with us. Norman came in from the studio and sat next to Mary on the sofa. After listening for a few minutes, he suddenly jumped up.

"Better get back to work!" he said, heading back out the door.

Mid-May

The end of the school year was coming up soon and everyone was more than ready for summer. I was walking down the hallway one day and thinking about the extra chores that Dad had planned for me after school, when I saw our principal, Mr. Moore.

"James," he said smiling, "tell your folks I'll be coming around to the house in the next week, I need to talk to them for a few minutes."

"Yes sir," I said, "I sure will."

At dinner that night, I told my folks what Mr. Moore had said.

"What did you do?" asked Ardis, passing a bowl of mashed potatoes to Joy, seated next to her, "break a window at school, too?"

I threw a roll at her head.

"Buddy!" my mom said, "stop that!"

Ardis stuck her tongue out at me.

"For cryin' out loud, Ardis!" I said.

"Ardis!" my mom said, "you stop, too!"

"Troublemaker!"

"Brat!"

"Meanie!"

"Baby!"

Edith and Joy sat at the table, looking back and forth between Ardis and me.

"Both of you! Stop!" my dad said.

"Ok," we replied together, eyeing one another for a moment before digging hungrily into our evening meal.

Late May

One early evening a week later, Mr. Moore knocked on our door and my mom showed him into the living room. She called upstairs to me to come down, and my father came in from the barn. We all sat nervously on the sofa and waited for Mr. Moore, seated on a sturdy chair across from us, to speak.

"I wanted to come by for a few minutes to talk to you about James," he started. "There's nothing wrong. As a matter of fact, everything's right. I thought you should know that his teachers – and I agree – think that James should really consider going to college."

I couldn't believe what I heard. I had always thought I would graduate from high school and work with my dad, and one day take over the family farm. College had never been a possibility in my mind.

"I know it can be expensive," he continued, "so I also wanted you to know that I will do all I can to help find him scholarship money to go. He's a good student, a good athlete, and I don't see any problem with that part being taken care of."

I looked up at my mom and dad's face and couldn't tell what they were thinking.

"Well," he said, standing up, "that's about it. Thanks, folks, and James, I'll see you at school tomorrow."

My parents thanked Mr. Moore and my mother showed him out. My dad stood there, deep in thought.

"Huh," he said finally, to no one in particular "imagine our Buddy in college." And then he walked back out to the barn.

My mother came to me and put her arms around me.

"Do what you want, Buddy," she said, looking up at me. "No matter what you decide – and it's your decision - we're proud of you."

I ran up the stairs where all three of my sisters had been leaning over the railing, listening. I smiled, then walked past them, whistling, and went into my room and shut the door.

College! Imagine that.

Early June

Art Becktoft had been liberated from the camp at Moosburg on April 28th and had come home on leave a few weeks later. He had lost a lot of weight while a POW but all in all, word was, he was ok. Art had stopped by to see us soon after getting back to Arlington, and I remember wanting to ask him a lot of questions about what had happened, but I didn't want to seem nosy. I figured when he was ready, if that day came, he'd tell me without my asking. Everyone thought of him as a hero, but he just shook his head any time anyone said that to him. Still the same Art.

Shortly after Art had come home, my dad was enjoying his daily morning chat with Norman.

"Whatcha workin' on, Norman?" my dad called through the studio door.

"Come on in, Jim," Norman had replied, "I want you to look at something."

My dad went inside and Norman started telling him how he had come up with a new Post cover idea while he had been listening to the news on V-E Day. The illustration was going to be called "Back to Civies," and it would show a soldier returning from the war, looking at himself in the mirror in civilian clothes that didn't fit anymore. Norman had had a bunch of local boys come over to model, but no one had looked right – they all were too healthy looking, their clothes fit just fine, and none of them looked like they had really been through a war. My dad agreed after looking at the photos. Norman didn't want to scrap the cover idea, but he wanted it to be right, too.

"I know who you should ask," said my dad, "Art Becktoft is in town, and I can go and bring him on over. He'd be perfect."

"If you think he'd do it, well, that would be great," said Norman back.

Norman didn't need to worry about Art saying yes, he was more than happy to pose for the illustration, like everyone in town who had a chance to model for Norman was. He always made his models feel like they were the most important model ever, and Norman truly was loved by everyone who knew him. He was loved not only for his work, but also for his kindness and his gentleness. But, funny thing was, Norman didn't seem to realize how folks felt about him, he was a very modest man. He also never really understood that we all felt honored to be selected to model, to be a part of his work, he was always real insecure about his painting. I can't count the number of times he would almost finish a painting and then trash it and start over, convinced it wasn't good enough. Norman was hard on himself, but I think being a perfectionist about every detail is a big part of what made his paintings so great.

My dad brought Art over to the studio later that same afternoon, and he stayed for just a bit to watch Art model. Art was wearing his uniform and had his duffel bag with him, Norman had asked him to bring them over to use as authentic props. Norman had suits in his prop closet left over from earlier modeling jobs and he had Art try them on, one after another. Finally, Art tried one of the suits on and the pants were way high, the jacket was too short. The sleeves were too short, too.

"Perfect!" said Norman, smiling.

Next, Norman took Art upstairs in the studio, where he and Gene Pelham had prepared a set. Bunches of ties were hung over a mirror above a dresser, but the 1942 Arlington High School ("AHS") pennant that's tacked up on the wall in the illustration was something Norman added on later, I guess because of us kids.

Norman knew exactly what he wanted Art to do – Norman always knew exactly what he wanted – and the modeling session went quickly. Before my dad could return to his chores, they were through, and Norman was handing Art his white envelope. There were no contracts, no modeling releases, nothing but five dollars and a handshake.

"Back To Civies" appeared just six months later as the December 15, 1945 cover for the Saturday Evening Post. By then, Art was back on active duty. He had met the girl of his dreams, Mary, an Army nurse at Rhodes General Hospital, Utica, and had married her two months before the Saturday Evening Post cover was published. They would be married for more than fifty years, until his death on September 28, 1996, at the age of seventy-seven.

Monday, August 6th

It's hard to know what to write about August 6th of 1945. Like so many other times during the war, our family was gathered around the radio listening to news reports breaking into regular programming. It was hard to understand the impact of what we were hearing.

"This morning, the United States military dropped an atomic bomb on the Japanese city of Hiroshima..."

Three days later came reports of another atomic bomb being dropped on the city of Nagasaki. The death toll from the two bombs ended up totaling more than one hundred twenty thousand.

Two weeks later, we learned Japan had accepted the United States's terms for surrender, and on September 2nd, Japan formally signed the surrender documents that ended the war in the Pacific.

The war was over. No more rationing, scrap metal drives, war bond efforts. No more practice plane spotting. It was so ingrained in all of us to live that way, it was odd to think we didn't have to anymore. But we left the railroad rail hanging up on the tree on the other side of River Road to warn of the enemy's invasion – just in case.

Saturday, August 25th

Tommy and I had had such a good time in New York the year before, we decided to make the trip again. We rode down with Bob Smith and this time we got around much easier. We took the subway out to see the Dodgers play a double header against the New York Giants. We continued to be the Dodgers good luck charm, and they won both games, eight to six, and then thirteen to three.

It was a much different ball club after the war was over, the older players that had been on the team during the war had retired and the younger players who had been in service came back. The stands were full again. It seemed that folks were looking for a reason to get back to normal and baseball was just the way to do it.

While Tommy and I were in New York, we stopped by to see Woody again, and we were greeted by a familiar face.

"Well, if it isn't Buddy and Tommy!" said the receptionist, smiling the same fake smile that had been plastered on her face the year before. "Have a seat and I'll get Mr. Woodman for you. It is *so nice* to see you again! And Buddy - *my* how you've *grown!*"

"About like the hair piled on top of her head," whispered Tommy under his breath to me as I sat there, politely smiling back at her, trying not to bust out laughing.

1946

Spring

I *had* grown quite a bit in the last six months. Farm work had strengthened me and it didn't hurt that I had tall relatives. Norman needed me for another Boy Scout calendar, and I was happy to do it.

The name of the illustration was "Men of Tomorrow," and it was the most involved modeling job I ever did for Norman. In it, there are seven Boy Scouts carrying two canoes downhill through the woods while a Cub Scout looks on. Tommy was too old to model for the Cub Scout like he had in Guiding Hand, so Norman used Peter, who was ten. The other seven scouts are all me. So that it wasn't so obvious, I have my head turned away in all of the poses but one. Norman used two similar poses of me under the two canoes. On the far right side, both upper and next to the larger canoe, he used the same pose, the profile of the left side of my face. The branches in the foreground and the canoes hid my knobby knees in most of the figures, but you can see that the legs are the same in the figure under the large canoe and in the Boy Scout leading the way.

With so many poses, the job took more time than ever before. To get the perfect angle of my legs and body coming downhill like they were in the illustration, Norman set up wood planks in the studio, and he tilted them at various degrees during the modeling session. He wanted to catch the muscles in my legs when they were really being used as if I were coming downhill. He had a full-size canoe in the studio and I had to hold it over my head, balancing it, just as it is in the illustration. When we were done, Norman had all he needed to complete the 1948 Boy Scout calendar.

Norman was great during the modeling session. Like always, he jumped around the studio and showed me exactly what he wanted me to do. He made the faces he wanted me to make, he held himself stiff in the poses he wanted me to pose. And all the time we were working, Gene took picture after picture after picture.

Peter wasn't in the studio while I was posing, Norman had him model separately. That was Norman's typical way – he treated each model like a different piece of a jigsaw puzzle that only he could put together. Even when he painted, he never seemed to have a plan in the way he did his illustrations, it was more like peeling away layers of an onion, only in reverse. I remember Tommy and I were sitting on the bench underneath the window one time, watching Norman as he worked. You couldn't tell what he was thinking. He'd finish one area and then switch to another completely different part of the canvas.

"Why do you jump around like that, Pop?" Tommy had asked. The Rockwell boys always called their dad "Pop."

"Well, I just do. It's not like watching a baseball game!" Norman said smiling, as he moved to another part of the canvas again.

Mid-June

With the war over for a few months, folks started thinking about having a good time again. It's hard to explain what it felt like, but it was almost like you wanted to enjoy every minute. We'd been through a tough time, and it took a little adjusting to not have the war be the starting point for everything – what you could do, what you should do, and what you couldn't.

But some things never changed, and haying season was one of them. Each summer, when the forage was ready, we started the haying. It took about six weeks to mow, rake, haul, and store the crop. Before 1945, we cut the crop by hooking a mower up to our team, Dick and Prince. We pitched the hay by hand onto wagons and hauled it back to the barn. We never baled our hay. Next, the loose hay was hoisted by a grappling hook and was raised up the outside of the barn using a series of pulleys and levers. We then released the hook and the hay traveled along a track until it dropped it into the hay mow, the upper part of the barn. It was stored in the mow until winter and then we pitched it down to the feed troughs for our herd.

Sometimes, we also used our Doodlebug. The Doodlebug was a vehicle that was half farm truck, half tractor. It had five gears that grinded loudly if you didn't have the clutch in all the way when you shifted. Sometimes we used the Doodlebug to help with the mowing, hooking it up like it was a team of horses, with someone seated on the mowing machine, raising and lowering the cutter bar by hand. Sometimes we used the Doodlebug to pull the trailers that we pitched the hay on, or used it to rake. It was truly an "all-purpose vehicle," long before that term became popular, and it made life on the farm a lot easier.

The Doodlebug was also the poor man's driver's education vehicle, and my dad was the unofficial driving instructor. All the kids in the Valley, including the Rockwell boys, were taught to drive by my dad, out in our field on the Doodlebug. He'd sit in the seat next to whichever local was behind the large steering wheel and patiently explain where the clutch was, the gas, the brake, and how to shift the gears. The Doodlebug, more often than not, would chug forward and the engine would die. My dad would pretend he was angry, but his eyes were smiling, and he would explain it all over again. Gradually, the "student" would get the hang of it and would celebrate by driving in circles over our bumpy field. We didn't know anything about a learner's permit, the adults in the Valley just sent their kids on over to Jim, and before you knew it, they were driving.

After the war ended credit was easier to get and we bought a Ford Ferguson tractor that really helped with a lot of the farm chores. We used it for haying, and we used it when planting, cultivating, or harvesting the crops and just about every other chore on the farm that we used to do by hand. It was a big advancement for our farm; saved us time and made us able to be more efficient in what we did. The after-war prosperity seemed to be a reality, even for rural Vermont farmers.

July

My grandmother, Elva Buck Edgerton, was kind of an odd woman, even if she was family. She never said very much to anybody, and her expression hardly ever changed. She wasn't a warm and loving woman like my mom was, and she didn't give us hugs and smiles the way you think all grandmothers do. She just sat outside on the porch all day when the weather was nice, and sat in the parlor all day when it wasn't. I don't recall a single real conversation we ever had growing up, even though we lived in the same house.

"She looks like she was weaned on a pickle!" Jerry had said about her one time, and though it sounds kinda sad, it was true.

It was probably that very quality that made Norman decide to use my grandmother as a model for one of his more famous Saturday Evening Post illustrations, "Going and Coming," which was published on August 30, 1947. The illustration is split into a top half and a bottom half. In both sections, there's a father driving an old car that has a wife, four kids, a grandmother, and a dog. In the top section, the parents and the kids seem alert and happy as they are headed facing the left side of the cover. The dad is sitting upright with a cigar in his mouth, the dog and one of the sons have their heads out the window, and one of the daughters is blowing a big bubble. And there, in the back seat, sits my grandmother – stone-faced and staring straight ahead.

In the bottom half of the illustration, the car is facing the opposite side of the cover, to the right. The dad is tired, the mom is sleeping, the dog and son don't look as excited, and the daughter looks bored. A banner hanging out of the window says "Bennington Lake," a fictitious lake Norman simply made up. And there, in the back seat again, sits my grandmother – still stone-faced and staring straight ahead.

I guess I have to give my grandmother credit for modeling for Norman, she posed for him three times in total. Like I said before, she was in "The Long Shadow of Lincoln," this Post cover, and in 1952 she modeled for a calendar Norman was painting for a Massachusetts Mutual Life Insurance Company ad. But of all three modeling jobs, and perhaps of any illustrations Norman ever did, no model was ever as perfectly cast as my grandmother was in "Going and Coming."

Wednesday, October 16th

As my father walked out of the barn, a big yellow school bus came

166

rolling across the covered bridge. He stopped what he was doing and watched as it came straight up the shared driveway between our house and the Rockwell's and made a slight turn behind their house. The lettering on the side of the school bus said, "Burlington School District." As my father continued to watch, about thirty children and a woman climbed off the bus and headed toward the studio.

My dad figured that Norman and Mary must have been expecting the bus, because normally no one in town would tell tourists where Norman lived. It was just understood by the townsfolk that if anyone was ever stopped and asked, they would point in the wrong direction, so that Norman and Mary's privacy wasn't bothered.

My dad couldn't help but walk around to the backyard and watch the children. They jumped around with excitement and freedom. They pointed up at our cows in the pasture, and enjoyed the wide open space in front of the studio window. Mary came out from the house, smiling, and stood next to their teacher. Immediately, the teacher clapped her hands and the children all quietly lined up, then filed into the studio behind Mary.

Inside the studio, the children were sitting in a circle on the floor as Norman patiently spoke to them about being an illustrator. One excited young girl, Alison, raised her hand politely several times, asking Norman how he got his ideas and his models. Norman enjoyed telling them all about how he normally used folks like us from around town. He let the kids look closely at his props and costumes, and they explored the studio from top to bottom. When their time together was over, he presented the class with a signed sketch and gave each child an autograph, then Mary gave each of them a red, shiny homegrown apple.

My dad was heading in from the pasture with the herd just as the kids were leaving the studio. Mary and Norman stood at the doorway, arm-in-arm, smiling. It was good to see Mary smile. She smiled more that day than my dad had remembered seeing in a while; many times lately she just seemed so darn sad. My dad raised his arm in greeting, and the Rockwells waved back. Then, the kids all started waving happily, too, to Norman, to Mary - and to my dad and our cows.

1947

March

Like I mentioned earlier, my sisters Joy and Ardis spent a lot of time with Mary – so much so that to this day, they think of her as their second mother. She was surrounded by a husband and three sons who didn't spend much time at home. Norman was always in the studio. Jerry often liked to be by himself, painting or wandering through the woods. Tommy was always with me, and most of the time we were at our house, either working with my dad or off somewhere hunting or fishing. As the youngest, Peter may have been home more, but it's not like he was doing things with his mom. So, having the girls around was a treat for Mary, too. Ardis was thirteen years old in 1947, the perfect age for learning about being a young lady from such a fine lady herself. And when Mary paid both Ardis and Joy to work in her house, it gave them a little pocket money, too.

One day while Ardis was over at the Rockwells, Norman came in and asked if he could borrow her for a few minutes. Ardis was happy to go out to Norman's studio, where he had Gene Pelham take a lot of pictures of her for a new Post illustration called, "The Babysitter." In it, a young girl is sitting in an overstuffed flowered chair, holding a screaming baby and a manual on how to babysit. She looks very frustrated as the baby pulls her bright red hair.

While Ardis posed for "The Babysitter," she didn't end up on the November 8, 1947 Saturday Evening Post cover, Lucille Towne was Norman's final choice. Lucille's family was well-known in Arlington. The family still lives there and now owns Chauncey's Family Dining on Route 7A, a self-proclaimed "family-owned casual diner with country charm." If you ever get down that way, the food and service are still as good as they were sixty years ago, and Lucille is around most of the time.

The baby in the illustration is none other than Melinda Pelham, Gene Pelham's daughter. During the modeling session, Ardis helped Norman out by holding onto Melinda and helped get the poses from Melinda – including the crying – that Norman needed. So, even though Ardis didn't get to actually be *on* the cover, she was happy she got to be the *real* babysitter, if only for the modeling session itself.

All these years, I never have asked Ardis how she got Melinda to cry, and she never told it, but whatever she did – it worked.

June

Norman deeply respected my mother. He saw how much she loved her family, which had grown to include the Rockwell boys. They had become "family by heart," as opposed to family by blood, and

169

she didn't see much difference. He watched, the way he noticed such everyday things, as my mother worked hard to support my dad's efforts and all of us without complaining. He often shook his head about the fact that she could shoulder a rifle or fill her fish basket as well as any man. It made sense, then, that when Norman had an important task to do, he would turn to my mother for help.

Norman's art editor at the Saturday Evening Post in the mid-1940s was Ken Stuart. When Norman got the green light to go forward with an illustration, he was often under a tight publication deadline to finish it and then the original oil had to be hand carried from West Arlington down to Philadelphia, to the Curtis Publishing offices. Long before companies like FedEx, the only way to quickly move important items was by personal courier. For Norman, the only person he entrusted with the canvas he had taken months to create was my mother.

Norman never gave my mom much notice, he would come over in the evening, pipe in hand.

"So, Clara, I need to get this illustration to Ken Stuart tomorrow…" he would start. My mom never said no, she was always willing to help out.

"Sure, Norman," she would say, smiling, "No problem." Then, after Norman left, she would race around the house in high gear to make sure everything and everyone was covered for the two-day trip to Philadelphia. She drove early in the morning to the train station in Albany and rode the train through New York City to Philadelphia, then took a taxi from the Philadelphia train station to the Curtis Publishing offices, all the while carrying the carefully packaged original illustration. It took the better part of the day, and after she had safely delivered her package, she spent the night at a hotel near the offices and rode the train home the next day.

My mom also modeled for Norman several times, including two published Post covers. The January 24, 1948 Post cover is called, "Ski Train," a cover that Norman did to kid about himself and how, even though he had adopted Vermont as home, he was still a flatlander when it came to doing outdoor things like skiing which was (and still is) so much a part of Vermonters' culture. Mom appears in "Ski Train" two times. She is the lady smiling behind the businessman, and the woman in the hat on the left in the hat, with blonde hair.

The shoot had a pretty elaborate set. Norman had actual train seats pulled out of a real railroad car and sent all the way from Albany to the studio. There were three seats shipped in all, and Norman set them up over by the fireplace in the studio to get just the right light. Like usual, Norman had several men model for the illustration, including Clarence Decker, but when the Post cover come out, Gene Pelham was front and center.

The other cover my mom modeled for was "The Gossips," but you won't see her anywhere in it. The cover, which was published on March 6, 1948, has fifteen faces, ten models from Arlington, two from Manchester, and Norman and Mary. The illustration shows folks spreading gossip. Starting in the upper left corner, a profile of one woman is seen talking to the profile of a second woman. Then, to their right, the second woman's profile is seen turned and talking to the profile of a third woman, and so on, until the last person on the lower right corner is the same woman who started it all.

Part of the idea for this cover came from Norman being amused at our party line phone system. Norman had put in a private phone line into their house before they even moved in, but he always smiled a bit if he was over at our house when the phone rang and all of us would stop dead in our tracks to count the rings.

"How do you know no one's listening in?" he had asked my dad one time when they had first moved next door to us, shaking his head.

"You don't," said my dad, laughing.

It was not his intention to insult any of the models by asking them to sit for this illustration, so because the idea of being a gossip was not the most flattering, he decided to include Mary and himself in the painting. But when it came right down to it, out of wanting to paint the truth as he knew it, he just couldn't bring himself to put my mom, one of the women he respected most in the world, in a painting called "The Gossips."

October

The students in the sixth grade class at Burlington's Taft School, who had come down to visit Norman, were having a hard time. Their smart, funny classmate, Alison Pooley, had died of leukemia the month before, on September 11th. She had fainted earlier in the summer, and within months, she was gone. The teacher, Miss O'Brien, thought it might be helpful to create a memorial to Alison. I don't know whose idea it was at the start, but the class decided that they would take up a collection and send it to Norman to see if he would send them a signed sketch that they could dedicate to Alison and hang on the wall. Alison had talked about the trip to see Norman a lot after they had come down to Arlington, and it seemed

172

the perfect thing to do.

The kids went around and asked their teachers, parents, and neighbors for donations, and they ended up with forty-eight dollars, not a small amount in 1947. They had their principal, Miss Cartier, send it to Norman, along with a note asking for his help.

When Norman got the letter from the class, it really touched him, and Mary, too. He was honored they had asked him to be a part of her memorial; Mary had been a schoolteacher of students about the same age as Alison – fifth, sixth, and seventh graders – in California before marrying Norman, and she loved children very much.

Well, Norman being Norman, he didn't let the class purchase a sketch. The next Spring, he returned all of their forty-eight dollars and along with it, he sent them the original oil painting of "The Babysitter," which had been published as a cover for the Saturday Evening Post on November 8, 1947. The kids used the forty-eight dollars to buy a plaque, and they hung the painting proudly on the wall of their school.

There's an important P.S. to this story that I think tells a lot about Norman and the greatness of the man, which, to be honest, was as impressive as the greatness of his artistic talent, so I'm going to tell you about it here.

In 1978, the same year Norman died, the Taft School was closed down. "The Babysitter" ultimately found its way to the Chittenden Bank in downtown Burlington, where it hung for almost twenty years. Then in 1996, the Burlington School District was having a hard time financially, and someone remembered that they owned an original Rockwell. The illustration had recently been appraised for three hundred thousand dollars and the school board thought they might sell it to a private collector to help out their budget. Most of the students from Alison's class still lived in the area, and when news of the school board's intentions was made public, they were furious. They felt that the illustration was not the school board's to sell, as it had been a gift to their class, not to the administration.

I was asked by a group of Alison's former classmates to serve on a committee to raise the three hundred thousand dollars to buy the painting from the Burlington School District so that the illustration could then be donated to a museum or some other public venue where it could be seen and appreciated, and I was more than happy to help. We called our efforts the "Save the Babysitter" campaign, and I'm proud to say we were successful in meeting our goal. "The Babysitter" now hangs in the Fleming Museum at the University of Vermont, where it can be seen and appreciated by hundreds of folks everyday.

Throughout the campaign, I had to make many media interviews and public talks. Everywhere I went, I was asked over and over why I thought it was that Norman had sent such an incredibly generous gift to a class of young students. I never had to think very hard about that question, and so I'll tell you what I told them – that's just the way he was.

CHAPTER SEVEN
WEST ARLINGTON, VERMONT
1948 - 1951

1948

January

It was hard to believe that I was already a senior at Arlington High School. I had gone after my school career the same way I had been brought up by my parents to live my life on the farm each day – be responsible, and whatever you did, do it right, or don't do it at all.

That's probably why I also became the school "bus" driver my senior year. We had bought Norman and Mary's station wagon a few years before when they got another car, and I started driving the West Arlington kids to high school each day. The car sat eight plus me as the driver. I got paid a dollar per week per person for the gas and the job, though my sister Joy didn't have to pay. The car was reliable, even though it didn't go in reverse easily. That didn't bother me much, you just had to make sure when you parked that you were facing in a direction where you could pull out straight ahead, just in case.

I had made a choice to be involved with the student government while at AHS, and at the end of my junior year had won the school election to be President of the Student Council for my senior year. I also had taken my interest in sports and put it to use in high school athletics. I played basketball and baseball throughout my entire high school years, and ended up Captain of both teams my senior year. I was also the President of the Arlington Athletic Association, along with Freeman Grout, who was Vice President; and Donald Crofut, who was Secretary-Treasurer. Freeman and Don were a year behind me, and Norman had used Freeman as a Boy Scout model when I got too old. But school was not all about sports, so I worked hard on my studies, too, and I graduated with honors.

Shortly after Thanksgiving, the Arlington High School basketball team was sitting on an old rented bus, headed home from a basketball game in Wilmington, a town forty miles away. The weather was not good, typical early December weather in Vermont. The roads were slick, and it was freezing outside. As we started to head around a curve on our way up the mountain just before coming into town, the bus suddenly skid to the side of the road and landed in a snow drift. The brakes had completely gone out.

Fortunately, we were all ok, but we were pretty shaken up at the close call. If the brakes had gone out on the way *down* the mountain instead of on the way *up* the mountain, no telling what would have happened. After a long day at school and a tough win in Wilmington, we held our breath as the driver got the bus back on the road and drove down the mountain in first gear.

The next day after school, I called an emergency meeting of

the Arlington Athletic Association to talk about the bus situation. The Arlington Town School District had just purchased a new school bus to transport students in grades one through eight who lived far outside of town. We decided to petition the town's school board if we could use the new bus for our sports activities after school. The bus wasn't being used in those times, it was just sitting at the elementary school, so it seemed a logical alternative. I wrote up a formal petition and Freeman, Don, and I attended the next school board meeting a week later and presented it.

Our petition, which we felt was not unreasonable, was met with total disdain by two of the three school board members. The chairman, Harlan Miller, did not believe in any varsity sports activities. He was the essence of a "milltown" owner who, literally, owned the town; a millionaire in those days, whether by marriage or his own efforts, I don't know. What I do know is that he was a lawyer, he owned a lot of property, and in short, he was a tyrant and a dictator. Harlan also had a small faction in town that always backed him up.

Chairman Miller leaned on his hands and was looking everywhere but at me as I stood and read our petition. He almost seemed to enjoy letting everyone at the meeting know how little he thought of my carefully worded petition. He looked smug, like one of our barn cats when it licked cow's milk off its face, and as I sat down, he looked over the top of his glasses and addressed me, personally.

"Buddy," he said slowly and sarcastically in his heavy New England accent, "you know, the *proper* way to have addressed this situation would have been to call a special town meeting."

"Well, sir," I said, trying to stay polite even though I would much rather have taken a swing at him, "how do we do that?"

"I don't have time to educate you young folks about how democracy works in the State of Vermont if you failed to learn that in your civics studies, Buddy," he said in a nasty tone. "You ought to be more mindful of your schoolwork, young man, instead of playing ball and such, and look up the regulations yourself."

My ears were already burning when he added, pompously, "Besides, there are no buses available because of a shortage. We were on a waiting list for quite some time before we got our bus."

Then he turned and chuckled at the other board members before continuing.

"But tell you what, son, if you can find one - I'll buy it."

And with that, they voted against our petition, 2-to-1 and we were shooed out of the meeting.

Freeman and Don were pretty down as we walked toward the parking lot, but my brain was going a mile a minute.

"What are we going to do now, Buddy?" asked Freeman, mindful that without safe transportation, our ability to have any sports activities with other schools was pretty much over.

"Well, boys, I guess we're gonna have to find us a bus," I said, walking a little faster and heading home.

Being naïve, but also partially wanting to call the Chairman's bluff, I had taken him at his word. The next day, I called a bus company in Albany, New York, and explained our situation and they delivered a bus in two days. They even parked it right where I requested it - directly outside Miller's offices.

Later I heard that when Chairman Miller looked outside and saw the new bus sitting there, he was absolutely furious, but I can't say that I felt bad about that. Not surprisingly, he also backed out on his promise to pay for it, so the bus company sent a driver over the day after they had delivered it, and drove it away. Still, it sat outside his offices for a day and made a statement in some way.

After that, I was pretty hot to deal with the issue. From where I sat, I had done my part. There was no way I was going to give up so easily. I called another emergency meeting of the AAA and we decided to call a special town meeting to see if the *town* would agree to let the athletes use the town's new bus in the off hours. So, taking Miller's comments about my lack of civic knowledge as a suggestion, regardless of how he meant it, I researched what we had to do.

Under the law, we had to get signatures from five percent of the registered voters in order to call a special town meeting. Right before Christmas break, I wrote the petition and all of the team members set out to gather the required signatures. The very first signature I got was Mary's, and the second was Norman's. Uncle Bob and Aunt Amy were helpful, too, and the town really supported us. We got the required five percent and we requested an informal interview before the school board the first few days of January, to formally request a special town meeting.

Chairman Miller's eyes actually narrowed when he saw me coming into the school board's offices.

"Son, I thought I made it clear this matter was settled," he practically growled the words at me.

"Well, sir," I said, as politely as I had ever been raised to do, "since we haven't had transportation for our sporting events, I've had more time on my hands, so I took your comments to heart, and used the time to learn more about civics. Specifically, about how to ask for a special town meeting. So, here are the signatures of more than the required five percent of the town's registered voters who would also like to have a meeting to talk about this a bit more."

I handed the stack of papers to the Chairman and tried hard not to smile, although I have to admit it was true delight to see how red his face got. To give you an idea, his face was about as dark a red as a Vermont barn is when it's newly painted.

I stood as still as I could, hardly wanting to breathe as the Chairman looked at the signatures. It almost seemed he wanted to find proof we had written them ourselves. He grunted a little and set the lined pages to the side, then looked over the petition itself. All of a sudden, his eyes lit up and he started to smile. I could feel my stomach start to turn as I waited for him to speak.

"Well, son, it appears you needed a bit more time for studying civics than you thought. You used the word 'direct' in your petition, not 'request.' This Board is not empowered to *direct* anything. So, looks like this petition isn't either. We're done. Now, you and your little friends there, run along home."

And with that, he made a big to-do about throwing our petition in the trash can next to his chair.

For a minute I couldn't move, I was so mad and humiliated. But even though I was disappointed, I wasn't defeated. When I got home, I sat down and talked with my mom and dad about whether to go forward or to let the situation go. My folks were proud and supportive of my efforts and told me they encouraged me no matter what my decision was. The next day I went over and talked at length with Mary and Norman and told them what had happened, word for word. Like my folks who had been quietly supportive, Mary was also calm and encouraging, but Norman was angry.

Looking back, it seems that he saw the bigger picture because of their different station in life. Here I was, a seventeen-year old young man, a poor local farmer, daring to take on the Goliath of a powerful local school board headed by a Little Napoleon who had no use at all for anybody questioning the Board's decisions or undermining his small town power. Both Norman and Mary gave me what amounted to a personal civics lesson on democracy. After talking for about an hour, Norman stood up, pacing in their parlor.

"Don't you dare back down, now, Buddy!" he said to me, waving his hands in the air to make his point. "You make up another petition fixing the words they said you wrote wrong, and I'll be the first one to sign it – even before Mary!" Mary and I both had to smile at that.

"This isn't right," he kept saying, "this isn't right. You can do this, Buddy. Go after them again! Circulate another petition! This is just like your dad, this is just like 'Freedom of Speech,' don't you dare let them push you around. *You*, Buddy, are a leader; *you* can do this. As a matter of fact, not only can you – you must!" he said, pounding his fist on the mantle. It was just about the most worked up I had ever seen Norman, and so very unlike him.

Mary and I had been sitting next to one another on their sofa, watching Norman as he had practically jumped around the parlor. Then, Mary turned and looked at me, and put her hand on my shoulder. She started to say something, stopped, took a breath, and then she said, smiling,

"Buddy, it's really very simple. It's about doing the right thing. And you – well, you *know* what that is. Now," she paused, "just go and do it, and know we'll help you any way we can."

By the time I went back home, I was so pumped up, I couldn't wait to redraft the petition. I rang up Freeman and Don and they came over to our house right away. Before the night was over, we had our new petition, and we started collecting signatures the very next day.

The new petition was even more successful in gathering signatures than our first one had been. We had clearly struck a chord with the townspeople, not just about the school bus issue, it had gone far beyond that when the local school board first tried to bat us away like a bunch of bothersome mosquitoes on the Battenkill. Mary had been absolutely correct about how she saw it – it was about what was *right*.

When I walked back into the school board's offices for a third time, Freeman and Don standing behind me, I didn't even try to hide behind politeness. I'm not saying I was rude, but I wasn't smiling, and I certainly wasn't calling Chairman Miller "sir."

"So, Buddy, looks like you finally figured it out," Chairman Miller said sarcastically, never even looking up from the papers. "Petition granted. The special town meeting to decide the issue of using *our school* bus for *your* fun and games will be held this Thursday, January 15th, at the high school gymnasium."

We were stunned. I guess I was half expecting the Chairman to come up with some other nonsense to block us, even if I knew we had done it right. Freeman and Don were all smiles and laughing, congratulating themselves and slapping each other on the back, but setting the town meeting so soon raised a red flag to me. I couldn't put my finger on it, but my gut said Chairman Miller was still trying to maneuver something, I just wasn't sure what it was. Then, it hit me – by setting the town meeting so fast, he figured less people would know about it, less people would come, and he could railroad this against us and be done with it once and for all. We had no choice but to go with it, so we left the meeting and started putting the word out about coming to the gym on the fifteenth.

The night of the special town meeting came, and I went with my mom, dad, Norman, Mary, and Tommy. We got there early and sat down near the front row of the bleachers. Not many people were there, and I felt my stomach start to get tight. But about fifteen minutes before the meeting was to start, people came pouring through the doors. In the end, more than seven hundred folks crammed into the school gym. Every seat was taken, and still more kept coming in, until there wasn't even enough room for people to stand. Famous author and educator Dorothy Canfield Fisher, an Arlington resident and close friend of the Rockwells, sat a few rows behind us. Her husband, John Fisher, served on both the local school board and the State Education Board. When I turned during the meeting to look around the packed gym, Dorothy smiled down at me, nodding her head.

The session was furious and angry voices echoed in the high-ceilinged room. Prosper Deschenes, the head of a local factory, was against us out of fear of Harlan Miller. Awful things were said about me, and about Freeman and Don. We were accused of being rebellious, of being troublemakers. Mr. Miller used his power as Chairman to monopolize the floor, trying to shut down the opposition, trying to keep any supportive voices from being heard, making long speeches that caused some folks to get restless and have to head out the door for home. I started wondering if we had been right to start the process, so many people seemed quiet. After two hours of speeches, mostly by the board members and its backers, the gym suddenly was totally still as the Town Moderator banged his gavel and called the vote. Each board member stated his vote out loud in both a grandstand move and one designed to intimidate the members by having them publicly take a stance.

"I vote nay," said Chairman Miller, standing, glaring right at me, before he sat back down.

"Nay," said Clayt Hulett, as he quickly stood and sat down, very short and gruff, almost like it was ridiculous he even had to state the obvious.

"Yea," said Harry Hayden.

The board vote stood at two nay, one yea. The Moderator next turned to the audience and asked everyone to cast his or her vote by a showing of hands.

"All those voting members of the community who are *for* the use of the new town school bus for the high school athletic activities, raise your hand!" he said in a clear, booming voice.

Norman's hand shot in the air first, quickly followed by Mary and my parents, Dorothy Canfield Fisher, and a few others. I held my breath as people looked at one another and then, suddenly, the entire gymnasium was a sea of hands held high in the air. Folks started cheering loudly, stomping their feet on the bleachers. Against the noise, the Moderator raised his voice.

"So noted! Nay?" asked the Moderator.

A few hands went up in the air, but they were insignificant.

"The ayes have it!" proclaimed the Moderator, smiling, as he slammed his gavel onto the podium.

Everyone jumped to their feet screaming out loud, waving their arms in the air.

I couldn't believe it! I stood there, shocked, then turned to my parents. My mother hugged me around the neck and my dad was clapping me on the back. From the podium, Harlan Miller had grabbed the gavel and was frantically pounding it, trying to gain control.

"Mr. Moderator, Mr. Moderator! *I hereby resign my position on the School Board, effective immediately, as does Mr. Hulett.* Ungrateful fools! I leave you all to the disasters of your own poor judgment!" he shouted with pompous anger.

Everyone *really* went wild then, cheering and jumping up and down, as Miller and Hulett made their way out the door. I couldn't believe it – we had toppled the town tyrant!

Everyone called "congratulations!" to me as they filed out of the gym. Dorothy and John Fisher walked past and John gave me the "thumbs up" sign. I looked to Mary and Norman.

Mary leaned over to me and whispered, "See, Buddy? It was the right thing to do."

Norman stuck out his hand and pumped mine up and down.

"Like father, like son," Norman laughed, as we all started walking to the door together.

"Yeah, except they *agreed* with him!" my father joked back, laughing.

A week later, a special letter dated January 22nd came in the mail to me. It was from none other than John Fisher, and it truly captures the times, though it seems his words still hold true even sixty years later:

"Dear Bud Edgerton:

I think it only fair to explain why none of your friends answered the attacks, made last Thursday night, on the students who had passed around petitions for the meeting. It was not because we had nothing to say, - on the contrary! But the main purpose of the meeting was to get a good majority, and I had already seen four voters from our party walk out as if they could not wait any longer….had to get home to look out for the fires or the children, I suppose. I was afraid that unless we speeded up the vote others might follow them…perhaps enough to cut our majority very thin, or even to beat us. So I kept quiet, and evidently no damage was done for, to judge from the vote only a few took Mr. Miller or Deschenes at all seriously.

But now it strikes me that perhaps you and others may run into criticism around town and might find the legal case I dug up convenient in answering. Or, even though no one ever questions your action, my notes still may be of value as they round out your practical experience with the study of American Civics. In my mind the work you and others did was a first class project in learning citizenship. I go to a great many educational meetings and listen to lots of speeches by famous educators. They are always talking about the need to get something into our course of study in the schools which will convince young men and women (soon to be voters) that Democracy is a good system and worth preserving. They also insist (on the technical side of teaching) that no amount of reading books has half as much education value of actually doing something which illustrates an important principle. I can't imagine any project which could have better fitted both these points.

186

It is clear that we can't hold a meeting every time a ton of coal needs to be bought for the Town Hall. Therefore we have boards of managers such as the Selectmen, and the School Directors. The legislature by statute gives the School Directors the 'Use of school property, and management of the schools.' 'Use' and 'Management' are fairly vague words. They do not make it clear beyond argument whether the Directors have full authority or whether they can be over-ruled by a meeting of the legal voters. That is a question for the Supreme Court, and so far as I can find out, the Court has never ruled clearly on the question. Some decision lean one way, some lean another. My opinion is that you did wisely to change the wording in your second petition to 'authorize and request' instead of claiming that we could 'direct'. I am not at all sure that a meeting cannot 'direct' elected officers, but there is at least enough doubt about their power to make it risky to claim more than we are sure about.

I am absolutely sure that it is proper to hold a meeting to request officers to change their policy, or to remonstrate with them. If anyone questions that tell him to read Article 6, Article 20, and section 67 of Vermont's constitution. You ought to read them yourself by the way. If you don't find a copy of our Constitution in the school library, let me know and I'll see that one is put there.

At first I questioned whether it was worth holding a meeting so near our regular March Meeting. Later I agreed with you that the moderate cost of a special meeting was well worth spending so that voters would have a chance to understand the issue and be ready to vote for Directors they can trust at the March elections.

As for the charge that you high school students were rebellious in circulating a petition to the voters, - that is just nonsense. The Town should (and the majority of the Town does) feel grateful to you for bringing it to their attention that our servants the Directors were not acting like reasonable men, but were insisting on a policy which even two very long speeches entirely failed to justify. The Directors have no power whatever over your actions when you are out of school and are not representing the school (as at some athletic game or sponsored dance, etc.). But even if they had such power, the facts are that when you petitioned them, you were told that the school bus question could be settled at a public meeting, and when the question was raised at that interview how a special meeting is called, the answer was you ought to look up the regulations about calling one. That certainly sounds like encouragement to go ahead and do what you did.

Mr. Deschenes, I remember, said that you had made Arlington the laughing stock among all neighboring towns. I disagree with that statement, as I disagree with everything else he said. If anyone should be ashamed of his part in the matter, it is Prosper Deschenes. I wonder if he ever heard of the Freedom Train. I wonder if he has ever read the great papers that train carried around the country. If he had read them he would have found that the Declaration of Independence, the U.S. Constitution, Lincoln's Gettysburg Address, speak of 'all men' of the 'people of the United States.' They do not say that 'these truths are self-evident' for everyone except for poll taxpayers, or that our government should be 'for and by' the larger tax-payers.

Of course we are all sorry that there is bad feeling in town. But the meeting did not create that bad feeling. It had been going on for several years. All that the meeting did was to bring it out in the open. And it's better to have a minority disappointed than to have a majority get more and more angry because it is never really listened to by its elected officers. Altogether I think Arlington voters owe you and your companions a vote of thanks for the courage and perseverance you showed in bringing the issue before the public. In the nine years I have served on the Board of Education school business has taken me into many sections of Vermont. I like the people I meet on these trips. I respect them. With very, very few exception they expect to stand on their own feet and they can't be bought. I was proud to find that my town, last Thursday, measured up with the rest of Vermont.

Cordially yours,
John R. Fisher"

February

Norman had created an illustration of a County Agent visiting a farm for a Saturday Evening Post article. It had been the idea of Art Editor Ken Stuart, and Norman traveled to Indiana to get just the right feel for the scene. He had added my dog, Shep, into the illustration after returning from Indiana. While working on the painting, Norman had asked my dad's opinion during one of their morning chats.

"Well," said my dad, "calves in the Spring aren't as fat as calves in the Fall, Norman. You might want to fix that. You also might want to put in some chickens scratching for food. Jessie Harrington up the road always throws out corn in the road and the chickens scratch pretty good, so you could get some pictures, I'm sure. Otherwise, it's lookin' pretty good."

Norman and Gene Pelham got the shots of Jessie's chickens and Norman finished the illustration. The image quickly became an important representation to County Agent Associations all across the country, and prints of the illustration are still routinely given at county agent awards ceremonies throughout the U.S.

Because it was so popular, Norman was asked to speak at the 1948 National County Agent's Association Annual Convention in Boston. As always, Norman was somewhat reluctant to do so. He liked talking with small groups, but speaking to large groups was never easy for him. But, at Mary's urging, Norman agreed.

The agents in the audience gave Norman a standing ovation as his name was announced. He spoke a short time before waving to the audience, and he left the stage to yet another standing ovation. The agents felt he had understood them; he had accurately painted scenes that related to their homes, their lives, their work. The respect and admiration for Norman was so strong you could almost touch it.

Just like Norman's illustrations, Norman was *real*.

Saturday, May 22nd

Norman was going to do a Post cover of the Chicago Cubs and he needed photos to work with. He invited me to go with him, Gene Pelham, and Tommy down to Boston to see a Braves game against the Cubs. The four of us drove to Boston and we stayed at the Kenmore Hotel, an expensive hotel in downtown Boston. I had never been in such a fancy hotel, and I tried not to look like a Vermont farm boy as we checked in, so I kept my head level and tried to look around the hotel lobby out of the sides and tops of my eyes, pretending I checked into hotels like that everyday of the week.

Tommy was totally comfortable in these surroundings, and he headed over and sat down hard in a big, overstuffed chair in the lobby as Norman finished checking us all in. A bellhop in uniform and wearing a small hat on his head came over to me and tried to take my bag, but I wasn't letting anybody take my bag; I was happy to carry it myself.

When Norman was finished at the counter, he turned and motioned to us and we followed him and Gene – and the bellhop, who was carrying everyone else's bags but mine – to the elevator. We went up to a floor near the top and when we got out, Norman took Tommy and me to our room, which was next to his and Gene's. There was even a door between our rooms, which I thought was pretty darn neat. As soon as we came in, Tommy ran over and leaped in the air and plopped onto the bed, fiddling with the radio on the nightstand, as I stood there not quite sure what to do. Finally, I sat down on the edge of the bed and looked over at Norman.

Norman reached in his pocket and gave the bellhop a tip and then came and sat down on the bed next to me. He looked over at Tommy and kind of chuckled, and then he turned and smiled at me. Norman had four quarters in his hand and he gave them to me – two for me, two for Tommy.

"Take Tommy and go downstairs," he said to me, "and get a haircut. Tell them to charge the room for the haircuts, and give the change to the barber as a tip. When you come back, we'll go

191

out to dinner."

"Ok, Norman," I said, still so excited just to be in Boston. "C'mon, Tommy, let's go." And with that, we rode down the elevators and got what was, to me, a very expensive haircut. It looked better than the haircut I got at the barbershop in Arlington, but for how much it cost, it should've.

After our haircut, the four of us went out to a restaurant near the water. I don't remember the name of it, but we all ate a lot – New England clam chowder, salad, a steak, and a fancy dessert. There were lots of people in the restaurant, and everyone seemed to be talking and laughing and having a good time. On the way out, Tommy and I grabbed a handful of mints in a little silver tray that sat by the cash register and stuffed them into our pants pockets.

The next day we got up and had breakfast in the hotel restaurant and then headed over to Braves Field. I was so excited I could hardly stand it. Even though it wasn't the Dodgers, it was still terrific – it was major league baseball! We got to go to the clubhouse and everyone there treated us like we were celebrities just because we were with Norman. I had just gotten a new Earl Torgeson mitt, "The Earl of Snohomish," first baseman for the Braves, and I got all of the players to autograph it. I used that mitt for years until it was worn out, autographs and all.

Even though it was great to meet the players and get autographs, the main reason we had come to the game was so that Norman could tell Gene what photos he wanted of the players, the people in the stands, and the dugout itself. While Tommy and I watched a few innings of the first game of the doubleheader, Norman was running around with Gene taking pictures. He was done before the game was over, and when Norman was done – it was time to go. Just like the movie we had gone to when I had modeled for "I Will Do My Best," Norman was on the run.

On the way back to West Arlington, we listened to the games on the radio. The Braves swept the doubleheader, eight-to-five and twelve-to-four. Guess Tommy and I helped the home team win no matter *what* stadium we sat in.

Early one morning a few weeks later, I headed over to the studio. As I approached the door, I had to step over my dog, Shep, who was lying right in front of it. Shep spent just about as much time at Norman's studio as he did at home. Pretty much, if he wasn't on our back step, he was on Norman's. As a matter of fact, there are a lot of photos in books on Norman showing him walking with "his" dog, but it's my dog, Shep, or sometimes my other dog, Spot.

"C'mon in, Buddy," Norman said, motioning, as he saw me reaching over the dog to grab the doorknob. He was sitting at his easel with a sketch of "The Dugout" pinned to the upper corner of the canvas.

"Hey, Norman," I said with as big a smile as I could, "how about if you come and talk to our student assembly about us going to Boston, and how you do your illustrations, how you work."

"Hey Buddy, how about if *you* tell them about us going to Boston?" Norman asked, trying to figure a way out of saying yes to my request without making me feel bad. Norman didn't really like to speak in public, even if it was only to a bunch of high school students.

"I don't think it'll be half as interesting if I tell *about* you instead of you coming, yourself, Norman," I said, trying hard not to sound like I was putting any pressure on him, even if I was putting pressure on him.

"Well…" he stopped and took a long draw on his pipe, looking up at me as I still stood there smiling, "alright, if you'll introduce me, I'll do it for you."

And with that, Norman agreed to come and talk about illustrating "The Dugout." When he actually spoke, however, he also mentioned how he had come to the high school to give the talk because we were neighbors and friends. That was a pretty proud moment for me - and it didn't hurt with the girls, either.

Late June

It was a beautiful day when the Class of 1948 walked down the aisle at graduation. Graduation Day in a small town is a big event, and the entire town turned out. My parents; sisters; grandmother; Aunt Amy and Uncle Bob; and Norman and Mary came to the ceremony. As President of the Student Council and President of the Senior Class, I spoke to my classmates about the bright future that was ahead for us all in the beginning of the post-war boom. We received our diplomas and, like so many others then and now, we cheered after we moved our tassels from left to right.

But all was not so happy in the Rockwell household. It seemed that Mary was frequently not feeling well, and she seemed to be smiling less than she had when they had first moved in five years before. She and my mother would talk for hours, often at the swimming hole, or sometimes Mary would come over and sit at the table and talk while my mother worked in the kitchen, canning food or cooking, or maybe even doing the laundry with our new electric washer. They were very close, I think at least partially because they were from such different worlds. Mary could let down and be real with my mother, and she respected my mother as much as Norman did. My mother's advice was frequently to work, that's what she had done to get through the tough times in her life, and it had been effective for her.

But while Mary worked very hard to help and support Norman and his talent - often running to the schools to get young students to model, or gathering props or costumes - working hard was not what Mary needed. Quite simply, she was lonely. Her sons were getting older and had their own activities, she had live-in help with the house, and Norman was in the studio seven days a week. Norman and Mary loved each other very much, that was obvious, but Norman also loved his work. And I think it's fair to say that while Norman would never have intentionally harmed *anyone*, having so much focus on his work meant he had less focus on his wife and sons.

Fortunately for Jerry, Tommy, and Peter, my mom and dad were pretty much surrogate parents, and my sisters and I were their siblings, too; and Norman often told my folks he was grateful for the place our family had in his sons' lives. And then there was Mary, somewhat isolated. In those days, we didn't know to call how she felt "depression," but it seems now that that's the battle she was fighting, and it was an unknown battle she fought alone.

Early July

I woke up excited, scared, happy, terrified, and curious all at the same time. Amazingly, I had been invited to try out for the Brooklyn

Dodger baseball system. One of their scouts had come to Arlington High School to see me play, after reading about my baseball record in the Bennington Banner newspaper. Doc Smith was going to drive my dad, Tommy, and me to Nashua, New Hampshire, for a pre-game tryout and night ball game. I couldn't wait. I had hardly slept the night before and was thankful for the adrenaline that kept me pumped up.

Doc came by in his big Buick early in the morning and we all piled in for the three-hour drive. Tommy and I sat in the back seat, talking. I didn't even dare to hope I would be chosen to play professional baseball.

We pulled up at the ball field right on time. Some other hopeful players were already beginning to warm up. I checked in with the coordinating coach and took my place on the field as my dad, Doc, and Tommy climbed into the bleachers to watch. For the next several hours, I stood in rotation with the other players auditioning, demonstrating my baseball skills as a first baseman. Finally, just before the night game was to begin, the coaches had all of us line up.

The tallest coach seemed to be in charge. He had walked around all day with a clipboard in his hand, making notes as we played. Now, he spoke to all of us.

"First of all, thanks for coming out and showing us what you've got," he said. "It takes talent to get this far, and guts to finish the day. You can be proud of yourselves simply for being here. But, our job – my job – is to select those of you who will go forward from here. So, as I call your name, please stand over here, beside me," he said, gesturing. "I won't be calling your names in any order, so please listen until I'm done."

I stood there, at first not realizing I was holding my breath. As the coach began calling off names, I looked up in the stands. Tommy was sitting there with his fists clenched, listening intently to the coach. When his eyes met mine, he smiled and gave me the thumbs up sign. I saw him nudge my dad and Doc, and they both looked over and grinned at me, too.

As the coach continued calling off names, I started having the feeling that when he had reached the end of the list, I would be standing in front of him, not beside him. I braced myself for the disappointment, while still clinging to the quickly fading hope that I would still hear my name.

"Well, guys, that's it. Thanks again for coming out. Maybe we'll see you next year. In the meantime, I hope you enjoy the game tonight!" the coach said, smiling.

The players who had been selected were excited and happy, and I walked over and extended my hand to each of them, then turned and walked toward the stands. It was hard not to let my feelings go, so I focused on putting one foot in front of the other, and found the strength to give my dad, Doc, and Tommy a big smile as I climbed beside them in the bleachers.

"That's a tough break, but, *next* year, Buddy, next year," said Tommy as I sat down, encouraging as only a best friend could be.

"Sure, Tommy," I said trying to smile, looking straight ahead toward the field to keep my composure, and knowing when I said it that there wouldn't be another chance, next year or any other year. But still, it was great to have had the chance to tryout for the Brooklyn Dodgers, knowing Doc, my dad, and my best friend were all there to cheer me on.

August

Shortly before I went off to college, things on the home front at the Rockwell's continued to deteriorate. Whether it was Norman or Mary that made the decision, I don't know, but Tommy and Jerry were sent away to the Poughkeepsie Quaker School, and Peter got to stay home. I was getting ready to go to college, and it was hard to say good-bye to Tommy, knowing he would not be there when I came home for holidays or just to bring my laundry home. But I'm sure that what motivated Norman was what was best for Mary. That's just the way he was.

September

I was accepted to Springfield College, but decided to go to the University of Vermont. I was the first person in my family to go to a four-year college, and I never would have gone if it were not for the encouragement of one person – Mary Rockwell.

As a former teacher, Mary had always believed in education and the opportunities it brought. When my mother had told her that the principal had come by and brought up the possibility of my not stopping with a high school education, it was Mary who solidly supported the idea. For the next four years after John Moore's visit, she and Norman both lobbied for my going to college with my parents, and Mary always encouraged me when she had the chance.

My mother was a bit more open to it; my dad, having had only a sixth grade education himself, didn't really see the need.

But somewhere along the way, Mary got it in my head that it was a challenge *I* wanted to meet. It became a given that I would apply to colleges and Mary helped me with that process, too. And when I wasn't sure what to study, she helped me figure it out.

"Well, Buddy," Mary asked as we sat in their parlor talking about my career choice for the umpteenth time, "what do you like to do most?"

"I like to help people," I said.

"So, what about being a doctor?" she said, smiling.

"Me? A doctor?" I was totally surprised at the suggestion.

"Sure, Buddy, why *not* you?" she said in response.

It sounded so simple when she said it. I had been wracking my brains trying to figure it out, but there it was – the obvious right choice. And that is how I came to be a pre-med major at UVM.

I pledged Lambda Iota as a sophomore, the oldest fraternity on campus. The frat house was – and still is to this day – on Pearl Street in downtown Burlington. It was a good bunch of guys, and a whole new world for me. The girls in the sorority houses were a whole new world, too. I jumped into campus activities the same way I had in high school, and worked hard at my classes. Problem was, I wasn't really cut out for pre-med, but it turned out that after all my years on the farm, I was perfectly cut out for agriculture. So, I changed my major to Agriculture Education.

There's another Rockwell connection to my going to college that I want to point out. Now, I know that there are many folks who maintain that Norman felt inspired to paint "Breaking Home Ties" when Jerry went into the Air Force and Tommy and Peter went off to school, but with all due respect, I just don't believe that's the case. Norman started painting the illustration in Arlington while I was in college. The illustration shows a young man and his farmer father on the running board of an old work truck, reminiscent of none other than our Doodlebug. And while it's true that in 1951, Peter had gone to a private boarding school, Putney School, as a fourteen year old; and Tommy had gone to Princeton, a private university, following his graduation from high school in 1951 (along with my sister Ardis); the painting was about a *farm* boy going off to a state school – note the "State U" pennant – and the thoughts of his farmer dad. That certainly wasn't Norman and his kids. Knowing Norman, and knowing that both he and Mary had to help convince my dad it was a good idea for me to go, that I was the first in my family to ever go to college, I feel certain this illustration was inspired by our family and my going off to the State University in Vermont.

Robert Waldrop, whom Norman had met while visiting the Boy Scout's Philmont Ranch, modeled for the young boy. Floyd Bentley modeled for the dad and Floyd's dog was the model for the dog in the illustration. While Norman finished the illustration in Stockbridge, he started it in his West Arlington studio using all Arlington local models.

Now, you may have recently read that this illustration was owned by the Don Trachte family and that Don – the illustrator who did the "Henry" comic strip – copied this painting and hid the original in a hidden compartment in his home, which was built by none other than my former basketball teammate, Ted Hoyt. In 2006, the original was discovered, and it was only then that anyone realized that the artwork believed to have been the original was actually a copy Don had made after his divorce to insure that his children, and not his ex-wife, ended up with the original. The irony is, Chris Schaeffer, Norman's business manager, had offered this Rockwell original and one other Rockwell original to my father first, for nine hundred dollars each.

"Jim," Chris said, "do what you have to do – mortgage the farm, get a loan, but I'm telling you, you really should buy these two paintings."

"I can't," replied my dad, "I need to buy a few head of pure bred cattle."

The original "Breaking Home Ties" sold at auction on November 29, 2006 for a record $15.4 million. When Dad sold his twenty-five head of cattle off in 1969, he got five hundred dollars per head.

1949

August

I had finished my freshman year at UVM and was getting ready to go back for my sophomore year. As I came out of the barn and was heading into the house, I saw a familiar car slowly crossing the covered bridge and driving up the common driveway between our house and the Rockwell's. As I walked toward the car, Tommy jumped out and came over to me, smiling.

"We're back!" he said.

"How was California?" I asked.

"Well, Hollywood High was ok, better than the Poughkeepsie Quaker School for sure, but Jerry got suspended for smoking, so he didn't finish this year," he said shaking his head and kind of chuckling.

Jerry and Peter were climbing out of the car just then and waved to me, and I waved back. Norman and Mary were busy pulling things out of the car.

"What's Jerry going to do now?" I asked in a soft voice.

"He's going to the Manhattan Art School," Tommy replied. "He loves art, too, and since having his own studio didn't work so well, Dad thought being in art school would be good for him."

"Well, Arlington High will be glad to have *you* back for two more years, their basketball and baseball teams really need you!" I said.

I walked with Tommy over to Norman and Mary and shook Norman's hand, gave Mary a hug. She was as pretty as ever, but I couldn't help but notice she looked tired.

"So Buddy, how about you and Tommy helping out an old man with these suitcases?" Norman asked, with a big smile. "I think you got bigger at college!"

"Sure, Norman, no problem," I said, "and welcome back. We missed you while you were in California, but I know my folks kept an eye on the place while you were gone."

"It's good to be back, Buddy, I missed the farm, and I missed your folks."

"Well, I know they missed you, too. And Shep kept going over to the studio and laying on the step, waiting for you to let him in. Actually, I think he's there now, I saw him over there this morning when I took the cows up the pasture," I said.

"Well," said Norman smiling, "I'll just have to go and open up the studio and let him in. Tell your dad to come by in the morning, we'll have a chat. I'm starting work on a new illustration."

"Will do!" I said, helping Tommy carry the suitcases in the house. When I left to get back to my chores, Mary stopped me on the way out the door.

"Come over later, Buddy," she said smiling, "and tell us all about how your first year at UVM turned out. And tell your mother I'll be by tomorrow, maybe we can go down and have a nice day together at the swimming hole. Good to see you, Buddy."

1950

March

I had been successful at UVM and was looking forward to finishing up my sophomore year. Norman had been asked to come to speak at UVM and I was excited to see him. He let me know he was coming, and we planned to meet on campus. I hadn't been back to West Arlington in a bit because it was tough to get a ride or hitchhike that far, and I was looking forward to having someone from home come up to Burlington.

At the appointed time, Norman and I met just outside the Ira Allen Chapel where Norman was to give his lecture. We gave one another a firm handshake that became a hug, and Norman started filling me in on all the local goings on at home.

"...So you'll never guess who might be following in my

footsteps," Norman said, smiling.

"Jerry?" I asked, thinking he had decided for sure he wanted to pursue his art.

"No, well, yes, he *is* interested in pursuing an art career, but that's not who I meant," he replied. "It's your young cousin, Jon Stroffoleno."

"Jon!" I said, "our very own 'barefoot Jon?' That really surprises me! He's always outdoors, building things or running around, I can't imagine him sitting down long enough to paint or draw."

"Actually, he's quite good," said Norman thoughtfully. "Your Uncle Bob mentioned to me that Jon is always drawing, so I suggested he take up a few lessons in town with Charlie Kagle. It's good to start at eight, nine years of age…"

We chatted on and on about other town happenings, enjoying the beautiful day, when all of a sudden a gentleman poked his head out of the big double doors behind us.

"Excuse me, Mr. Rockwell?" he asked, somewhat embarrassed, "I'm sorry to interrupt, but, uh, well, any time you're ready to start your speech, we'd, uh, be honored to have you come inside."

Turns out, while Norman and I had stood outside catching up on home news, he had kept an entire auditorium of folks waiting.

"I'll be right along," he said to the young man, trying not to laugh, then he turned to me. "So, come by next time you make it home, Buddy. It'd be nice to have a chat. Been a while."

And with that, he smiled and half waved, as he disappeared through the double doors.

That's just the way he was.

May

While I was away at UVM, my sisters Joy and Ardis became increasingly closer to Mary. They not only continued to work in the Rockwell house as they got older, and were frequent babysitters to Peter, Mary trusted them enough to let her guard down when around the two of them. She would talk freely about her thoughts, including her "church hopping" phase where she went to a different denomination every few weeks, none of which gave her the peace and serenity she was looking for.

Norman had a solid relationship with several other artists who had moved to Arlington – Mead Schaeffer, Jack Atherton, Don Winslow, and George Hughes. Don Trachte was also a close artist friend. The artists not only critiqued one another's work, they also socialized a great deal. But where Norman was friendly, funny, and wanted everyone's opinion, Mary began to withdraw more and smile less.

My sister Joy remembers one night in particular that she first saw Mary starting to struggle under the weight of what her life had become. Joy was in the kitchen of our house when Mary walked in – which was typical for our families, no problem. My parents were upstairs asleep already. Mary greeted Joy warmly and walked over to our liquor cabinet and poured herself a drink.

"Norman is busy with people," she said sadly, waving her hand in the direction of the studio. And with that, she sat at the kitchen table with my sister and had her drink, and talked into the night about books, the most comfortable subject she knew.

Fall

In 1946, the one room schoolhouse had closed for good. When the school board tried to sell it, they found out that my father owned the land it was built on, so it actually was *his* school – not theirs. My dad, wanting to support the town, quit claimed the schoolhouse and two acres of land over to the town, and no money exchanged hands.

For several years, the schoolhouse sat empty on the Green. Then, the summer of 1950, Norman decided it would be the perfect spot to create a studio for promising young art students. The schoolhouse was modified to have a dormitory and work space, and six students moved in, excited to work with such a famous illustrator.

One of the six students was Don Spaulding. Don was in his early twenties and had been a member of the Art Students League when he had been given the opportunity to study with Norman. After a summer of living at the schoolhouse, he was so taken with the area that he bought a house in a nearby town, Dorset. Even though he had moved a few towns over, he still came back to West Arlington to visit.

When Don got a contract to illustrate the Lone Ranger comic book series for Dell comics, he asked Norman to get in touch with me, to see if I would like to model for the covers. Being paid to model was easy money and I was a college student, so I jumped at the chance. I modeled for fifteen Lone Ranger comic book covers for Don. His process was very much like Norman's – first, he took a photograph, then he worked from the photo to the final piece. It was easy to see Norman's influence on Don's work.

It was a great experience to be able to model for the Lone Ranger.

Though I had handled guns all my life, there sure is something different about holding two pearl-handled revolvers while you're dressed up like a cowboy – no matter how old you are.

1951

February

Mary's depression had worsened over the cold Vermont winter, and she and Norman decided it would be best to start getting treatment at the Austen Riggs Center in Stockbridge for her depression. She commuted back and forth on a regular basis, but did not appear to be getting better. My mother was distressed that Mary had chosen to get treatment at a private clinic instead of a non-private one.

"If she went to a regular doctor, she'd get better faster," she said to me more than once, shaking her head. "Those private hospitals don't have any motivation to get her well and every motivation in the world to keep giving her expensive treatments."

Fourteen-year old Peter had been sent to Putney Day School in Putney, Vermont, for school that year, and Jerry was old enough to take care of himself. It was Tommy's senior year at Arlington High, and he jumped into his schoolwork and sports with tremendous enthusiasm. He also spent a lot more time at our house, helping my dad with chores. It seemed to suit him, comfort him, to work alongside my dad and to take meals with us. My folks were warm and gracious people, and they regarded Tommy as one of their kids. When Norman and Mary had to stay over in Stockbridge, Jerry and Tommy stayed with us. It was just understood – whatever the families needed, we were there for one another.

Norman worked longer hours than ever in his studio, still enjoying his morning chats with my dad. But his eyes were sad as the months wore on, and our hopes for Mary's recovery were growing more dim.

June

Ardis and Tommy graduated from Arlington High School and all of the Edgertons and Rockwells were there to celebrate together once again. I had come back from UVM in time to watch my baby sister get her degree, the fourth Edgerton student to graduate with honors. Tommy was Valedictorian and Ardis was Salutatorian of the Class of 1951, and it was a proud moment for all of us to see their successes.

Just after Ardis and Tommy graduated, Jerry joined the Air Force. Jerry was a great guy, a great friend, but he didn't have much direction at that point, and the military seemed ideal for him. He had tremendous artistic talent, but he hadn't found his stride yet. Just before he shipped out, Norman asked him to pose one more time. Jerry hadn't modeled for Norman as much as Tommy or Peter had, partly because he couldn't sit still that long, I suppose. Jerry was always a bit of a dreamer, and his attention was easily caught by his surroundings.

For this illustration, Jerry had to look a little sketchy. He portrayed a tough kid, sitting at a table and watching an old woman and a young boy praying in a rundown restaurant near a train station. The illustration, "Saying Grace," quickly became one of Norman's most famous and best-loved illustrations. While the original ended up in the private collection of Ken Stuart, the art editor at the Saturday Evening Post, the preview ended up in my sister, Joy's hands.

Joy was two years younger than I was and had graduated from Arlington High School with honors in 1950. She had decided to go to dental hygienist school in Rochester, and to help pay her way she worked as a nanny for the Sterling family. The Sterlings were very good to my sister. They had two young sons, Stu and Jack, whom Joy looked after in exchange for room, board, and a small weekly allowance. Shortly before "Saying Grace" was published as the Post cover of November 24, 1951, Joy had gone over to Norman's studio. Ardis trotted along, too. Joy had wanted to give the Sterlings a special Christmas gift that year.

"Norman?" she asked, "would it be possible for me to have one of your sketches to give to the Sterlings for Christmas? And would you sign it?"

"Sure," he had replied, pointing toward a stack of sketches on the bench under the front studio window, "look through those and take one you like for the Sterlings and keep one for yourself, how's that?" he asked, smiling.

"Thanks, Norman!" Joy said.

Joy went over and slowly, carefully looked at the beautiful sketches, many of them full previews of Norman's originals. Each one was more wonderful than the next, and Joy was excited to have something so precious to give to the Sterling family and for herself.

While Joy was looking through the pile, Ardis walked over to Norman. She smiled and asked politely,

"Norman, could I have one, too?" she asked. Ardis was never one to be shy.

"Sure, Ardis, help yourself. Any one you like," Norman said, smiling at her.

Joy decided on the preview for "The Babysitter" for the Sterlings, since she was their babysitter and "Saying Grace" for herself. Ardis picked "Santa Looking At Two Sleeping Children," a favorite Christmas illustration.

The girls crossed the studio with their choices and Norman smiled as he wrote, "To My Friend Ardis Edgerton, Sincerely," above his signature on the Santa preview; he repeated the same for Joy.

Years later, Joy and Ardis donated their previews to the Norman Rockwell Museum, as I did with my preview of "The Guiding Hand." We had had no idea at the time Norman so freely and easily gave us pieces of his work how important and valuable those previews would be to thousands of Rockwell admirers. He was just Norman, our next door neighbor, our friends' dad, our parents' friend. He was generous to a fault, and a fair man, happy to help my sister Joy to do something nice for people he had never even met.

That's just the way he was.

Mid-August

It was hard to believe that I was starting my senior year at UVM. I had been elected as the President of Lambda Iota fraternity and had been an honor student all the way through school. I really enjoyed the college experience and embraced it totally, taking full advantage of all that campus life had to offer.

I was lucky that we had the money for me to go to school that year. A fierce storm had lashed New England in November 1950 with a powerful fury. Vermont had been particularly hard hit. We lost fifty percent of our wood lot to the wind and torrential rains. After the storm passed, the trees on our wood lot looked like a pile of broken matchsticks.

After our hay crop was harvested, Dad and I worked at salvaging the downed timber. We worked our horse team and tractor overtime to cut and haul the logs to landings, where the logs were loaded onto trucks and delivered to local mills. The money we made from the unexpected timber harvest paid for my final year of college.

I can't say that I took any pleasure in losing the timber. But, if the storm had to happen, it was nice that I got a year's education out of it. Sometimes you just don't see how things are going to work out, but somehow they always do.

West Arlington (October 2, 1953) - Dot came to visit West Arlington (and my family) for the first time. We were married less than a year later.

CHAPTER EIGHT
WEST ARLINGTON, VERMONT
1952-1953

1952

Saturday, June 15th

It was hot and steamy in Burlington, Vermont. The temperature was hovering around ninety degrees, and the air felt heavy with the promise of an afternoon rain. I had gotten up just before sunrise, a habit from years of working on my family's dairy farm, preparing for the big day ahead. It was graduation day at the University of Vermont.

Looking out from the window of my third floor room in the frat house, I could see cars starting to line up along Pearl Street. Even the sidewalks had more folks than usual, students wearing caps and gowns, ladies wearing gloves and Sunday dresses, men in suits and straw hats, some of them carrying umbrellas just in case. I spotted my roommate, Norris Elliott, running up to a pretty girl and swinging her around, laughing, before heading hand-in-hand

213

in the direction of Memorial Auditorium downtown. Everyone seemed to be in good humor, talking, waving at friends. You could feel the excitement, the same way you could tell when a summer thunderstorm was coming, even though the sun was shining. You could just feel it.

I turned from the window and walked to the far side of the room and sat on the edge of my bed, trying not to mess up the cap and gown that I had ironed and carefully laid out just a few hours before. My emotions were all jumbled up inside. Even though I had enjoyed being at UVM, I was happy to be done with the work of being in school, ready to put the responsibilities of assignments and tests behind me and eager to take on the responsibilities of moving forward into the "real world." And yet, other than the farm, this room was the only other home I had known. It was safe. It was familiar.

I glanced around the room. Two suitcases stood neatly at the doorway in preparation for my trip to West Arlington early the next morning. I was going to drive my green '33 Chevy first thing, heading down Route 7 to home. It would take me about four hours. I'd arrive in plenty of time to settle in at my folks' house and then help my dad bring the cows in from the pasture before sundown.

Other than the suitcases, the room was pretty much empty, in an odd way. It was so empty it almost echoed, which was a long way from the ruckus that had normally gone on in our room.

I looked down at my watch – 11:33 a.m. I needed to hustle a little bit, I was meeting up with my mom and dad and I hated being late. They had driven up to Burlington that morning for the graduation ceremony, and we were going to lunch before Commencement started. Standing up quickly, I crossed to the mirror over my now-empty dresser for a final check. My tie looked slightly crooked. As I reached up to straighten it, I could hear my dad patiently explaining how to tie a single Windsor knot.

"...then pull the wide end through the loop again and down through the knot in front..."

I wondered what my life would look like when I got home to the farm. I wondered how long it would be until I got married and had a son of my own to teach how to tie a tie. I wondered if I would do as good a job raising my family as my dad had done raising all of us. And with that thought in mind, I looked at myself one more time in the mirror, took a big breath, and walked into the hallway, slowly closing the door to my youth.

July

Early in the morning, my dad came down the lane from the pasture and stopped at Norman's studio door.

"Whatcha workin' on, Norman?" he called, like he had every morning for more than ten years.

"Come and take a look," Norman replied, as he always did.

My dad walked in and saw a portrait of President Eisenhower on Norman's easel. As he walked around the room, my dad let out a low whistle.

"Wow, that's amazing," he said.

"What is?" asked Norman.

"Well, no matter where I go in the room, Ike's eyes follow me," said my dad.

"Hmm," said Norman, getting up and testing my dad's theory.

"How do you do it, Norman?" my dad asked.

"I don't know, Jim, it's just something I learned," Norman said, shaking his head. "I just try to do it right and it seems to come out ok."

Modest to a fault; that's just the way he was.

August

When my Uncle Bob and Aunt Amy got married, their babies came quickly. A year after their wedding, Jo was born; eighteen months later came their first son, Jon; Beth followed in 1944 and Fay arrived in 1947. Bob worked hard to support his family. In addition to being a gifted mason, he also earned money working for Norman doing odd jobs. Bob could fix anything, build anything. Many times, Norman also used Bob and Amy's dog, Gent, in his illustrations. He'd "hire" Gent to model for him and when he was done, Norman simply opened the door and Gent found his way home up the road. Norman thought highly of Bob, and Bob likewise thought the world of Norman.

It was funny, Bob and Amy's four children were just like my sisters and me – first a daughter, then a son, followed by two daughters. And, like me, Jon was "all boy." But unlike me, Jon was very inquisitive, very restless. He was like a modern day Huck Finn – always barefoot, always cooking up ideas, his hair disheveled, his large eyes brightening at the thought of each new and, as yet, undiscovered adventure.

Jon showed a knack early on for being mechanical just like his dad, frequently taking things apart and putting them back together, usually successfully. He even built a six foot by six foot clubhouse, complete with a roof and working door, at the mere age of ten. Jon was also a gifted artist. In school, he often sketched airplanes - fighter pilots and Messerschmitts - or detailed pencil drawings of deer and trout. He was the best student in his class, advanced over the other kids in his class, but he was always humble about it. Everybody loved Jon; it was hard not to. He had a perpetual scrape on his knee and a permanent grin on his face. That was my cousin, Jon.

Jon was ten years old in August of 1952, he hadn't had his birthday yet, that wasn't until November. Jon's best friend at the time was Martin Oakland, but everyone called him Marty. Marty was an adventurous sort, a kid who liked to pretend about swashbuckling pirates and heroes. One sunny summer day just before school started up again, Marty and Jon were walking along and trying to think what to do. The air was hot that day, more humid than usual for the valley. The boys had been looking for something fun to do to escape the heat and Marty had come up with the idea to ride down the Battenkill River on an abandoned barn door they'd found. At the time, it made perfect sense to the boys. They weren't mindful of the Battenkill at that time of year, swollen from recent summer rains. They wanted to be like Huckleberry Finn and sail down the river to the Hudson or some far away place, so off they went.

Jon and Marty balanced the barn door carefully on their heads as they marched very deliberately down the road to a clearing at the river's edge. They eased the door into the water upstream from the Covered Bridge and hurriedly climbed on. The current was pretty swift, and it quickly took the barn door out to the center of the river. In no time at all, they were floating downstream. Everything was going according to plan except that it was really, really hot. So, instead of sailing to the Hudson River and the ocean beyond, Marty suggested that they beach the barn door at the covered bridge and go swimming instead. The boys maneuvered the barn door close to the bank and Marty jumped off, pulling it up onto the grass.

"C'mon!" he shouted over his shoulder to Jon, as he raced around the bank and to the side of the covered bridge, "let's jump!" And with that, Marty climbed on the railing and flew into the water.

Jon started to follow Marty and paused for a moment.

"Jump!" said Marty, coming up out of the water and looking up at Jon, still hesitating.

Jon slowly and carefully climbed up on the railing and, closing his eyes tightly, he jumped off. Marty watched as Jon hit the water, and then waited for him to come up. Jon didn't. Marty started to realize there was a problem, when Jon suddenly broke through the surface. He was waving his hands around in the air and he looked terrified.

"I can't swim!" he yelled to Marty.

"Doggie paddle, Jon! Doggie paddle!" said Marty, starting to swim over to help.

"I can't! I can't!" he yelled, and Jon went under the water again, thrashing his arms around, grabbing at the water.

"HELP! HELP!" yelled Marty. "SOMEBODY HELP! HE'S DROWNING!"

A utility lineman had been working on clearing some brush nearby and he came running, as did Don Winslow, who bolted from the one-room schoolhouse. By this time, Jon had not come back up out of the water. The lineman reached down and took off his work boots and dived head first into the water. Miraculously somehow, he found Jon underwater, unconscious, and he pulled him out of the water and laid him on his back on the grass. By then, Don had made it to the river's edge.

Jon wasn't moving, wasn't breathing, and his lips were blue. The lineman began pressing hard on his lungs, and nothing was happening.

"C'mon!" the lineman yelled, as he continued to press on his lungs, "c'mon!" Frustrated, he literally began pounding on Jon's chest as Marty and Don held their breath.

Suddenly a huge gush of water literally flew out of Jon's mouth. He coughed and coughed, then all of a sudden, he sat straight up and looked around at all of them, as they were looking at him, obviously scared and upset.

"Guess I should've told you I couldn't swim before I jumped," Jon quietly said to Marty.

Late August

Tommy left for his freshman year at Princeton and fifteen-year old Peter went back to the Putney School, in Vermont, for his second year. Jerry was still in the Air Force and was stationed in Korea. I had joined my dad working on the farm and, using what I had learned at UVM, felt it was important to expand our revenue base beyond our herd. One of my decisions was to start raising chickens. Nowadays, folks call chickens raised like we did "free range chickens," but to us in Vermont in 1952, it was just plain raising chickens.

Here's how it works: There's a range shed where the chickens live that's on runners. It can be moved to allow the chicks to have different places to forage grass or clover, in addition to our feeding them grain. Water is piped into water troughs for them to drink. After the chickens run around all day, you have to gather them up each evening and put them back into the range house. The range is surrounded by chicken wire to keep the chickens in and the raccoons out.

One morning when I went to let the chickens out, I saw that one of the chickens only had one leg, and that meant a raccoon had tried to pull it through the fence. I took Shep out the next evening and Shep got the scent of the raccoon pretty quick. He treed the raccoon and I shot it with a .22. I was very protective of my chicken empire-to-be.

We had about three hundred chickens in total, mostly capons and broilers. When I sent a batch to slaughter, I always gave Mary ten halves - her cook loved to cook my fresh chickens! We delivered the chickens in crates to a poultry dressing facility called Reed Farm that was located in Dorset, a town about ten miles away. They were returned to me de-feathered and put on ice. I had to pick them up within a few hours from dropping them off and then sold them to local markets. Our capons, we sold to a Boston market (and no, I'm not talking about the fast food chain). Their buyer had trucks and crates, so they took the chickens live. The business was ok, it did provide some additional revenue, although not as much as I would have liked. It was a labor-intensive operation.

One evening as my dad and I were starting to crate the chickens to relocate them to the field range, Norman came along River Road on his evening walk. His walk took him right to the barn where we were rounding up the chickens.

"What're you doing?" he asked.

"Well, we're catching these chickens," my dad said, "and putting them in there." He indicated toward the crates.

"Hey, I'll help, if you like," said Norman.

"Sure, uh, ok. Well, see, uh, all you have to do is catch the chickens and then put them in that crate, and that's it," my dad said, wondering how this was going to work. "Thanks, Norman."

Well, I don't know how to say this delicately, so I'm going to try to talk around it. When chickens have been eating all day, the food moves through their digestive system, and they "release" it in droppings. As a result, the area where the chickens are is pretty dusty, and the dust is pretty much pure…digested material, shall we say? Norman, never having grabbed chickens before, didn't quite know how to go about it, so he started running around, chasing after the two pound birds, his hands low to the ground like he was going to scoop them up. And the chickens, wondering who this person was chasing them, got spooked and ran frantically in circles, anywhere, to get away from Norman. The more Norman ran after them, the more the chicks spread out, and dust and feathers were flying into the air. My dad and I just stood there watching as he kicked up an awful lot of "chicken dust." Sometimes, he got so excited, he would run after a chicken, only to slip and fall down, getting covered in…chicken dust. So, there he was, running around for about ten minutes, as we stood there trying not to laugh, and finally, finally, he caught *one* chicken. He held it out in front of him and proudly walked over to the crate, then placed it gently in the container, and turned around toward us, smiling triumphantly. He was a sight, covered from head to toe in dusty droppings, feathers stuck to his clothes and in his hair.

"One down, two hundred ninety-nine to go," my dad said to Norman, straight-faced, but with his signature twinkle in the eye. I couldn't hold the laughter in anymore and I started laughing so hard, I almost fell down.

"Well, Jim" said Norman, straight-faced back and shaking his head slowly as he pulled his pipe out of his pocket, then seeing it was covered in dust, slowly putting it back in his pocket, "I guess I'm never gonna make it as a chicken farmer."

And with that, he proudly continued on his evening walk, dusty, but happy he had helped us catch one token chicken.

Monday, November 10th

Autumn arrived on schedule and brought with it the annual foliage spectacular. The changing leaves turned the valley into a sea of crimson reds and brilliant oranges and yellows. Halloween came and went, and a chill filled the air with the hint of Winter.

I was bringing the cows in from the top pasture, headed back toward the barn, when I saw my father walking toward me. As he got closer, I could see from the look on his face that something was terribly, terribly wrong. My mind raced in an instant, wondering what it could be – my grandmother? Mother? Perhaps one of my sisters?

My dad looked at me, tears just on the edge of his eyes, and he tried to talk, but no sound came out. I braced myself for the worst, I had never seen my father like that. I suddenly realized I was holding my breath, waiting for him to speak. When he finally managed to find his voice, it was shaky.

"There's been an accident," he said slowly," a hunting accident, and...Jon's gone."

My legs gave way at the news, and my father took me in his arms as I wept. I took a deep breath and slowly wiped the tears from my face. Together, my father and I led the cows to the barn; regardless, the farm chores still had to be done. Downcast, we crossed over the lawn and went inside to my mother and sisters. More than any other time I can remember, that day, family was everything.

The sense of shock, irony, and pain remains for all of us, even fifty-seven years later. It is still unthinkable that Jon would have so narrowly escaped death in the river, only to lose his life three months later, and just two days after his eleventh birthday. But, we don't talk about how it happened, and we won't talk about how it happened now. Like I said before, that's not how folks in Vermont handle things, and the "how" doesn't matter anyway. There never was and never would be any blame, no need for discussion. All that mattered was that this terrific boy, whose life was saved in August, was lost to us after all.

A few days later, family and friends, including Norman and Mary, gathered at the West Arlington Methodist Church to pay their last respects to my young cousin. It was a beautiful New England day, warm for mid-November, as I recall. The sky was clear, blue, with wispy white clouds, and the sun shone brilliantly. There was no breeze, it was still, quiet. It was as if even the heavens were being respectful as we laid Jon to rest.

My Uncle Bob and Aunt Amy were strong, stoic. They stood,

hand-in-hand, silently. The love that flooded the church sustained them, and somehow, everyone got through that day and the days that followed, moment by moment. I learned some days later that after the funeral, Bob had gone up the mountain behind his house and had smashed the gun against a tree, until there was nothing left to it.

As with all of Bob and Amy's friends, Norman and Mary were sadly touched by Jon's death. A few days after Jon's funeral, I was heading into the house from the barn, when I saw Norman walking up the dusty country road from where our houses sat, headed toward Bob and Amy's. I waved to him as he went by, but I guess he didn't see me, he just kept going. He walked slowly, deliberately, his signature pipe in his mouth, a package wrapped in brown paper neatly tucked under one arm.

Up the road, Bob was sitting on the front steps of his house. His chores were finished and his heart was heavy, and he had gone outside in the fresh air to be alone for a few minutes. Amy was in the kitchen, making dinner, not that Bob had much of an appetite. He had just picked up a knife and small piece of wood, and began whittling - nothing special, just to keep his hands busy – when his attention was suddenly caught by the sight of Norman, walking up the steep driveway and across the flagstone steps to their modest house. Norman hesitated, and Bob shifted to the right, gesturing for Norman to sit on the stone step beside him. They sat silently, side-by-side, looking out over the yard, the air still and the sound of the Battenkill making a whooshing sound as it rolled over the rocks.

Without saying a word, Norman took the brown wrapper and extended it to Bob.

Norman stammered quietly, "I'm sorry it's not so good; I did it from memory."

As Bob slowly opened the brown wrapper, he was stunned to see a beautiful, charcoal portrait of his precious son, Jon. He did his darndest to hide his tears. The portrait was a profile view, not Norman's typical pose, the eyes soulful, the mouth gently closed.

Bob tried to talk, but no words came out, until he finally was able to whisper his thanks. With that, Norman looked down and smiled, then stood up, nodded, and slowly walked back down the country road to the haven of his studio.

Jon's portrait proudly hung on the knotty pine paneling of my aunt and uncle's living room. For almost sixty years, the family has kept the gift from Norman private, comforted by its beauty, and appreciative of Norman's heartfelt gesture of friendship. The portrait itself is special since, unlike all of Norman's other paintings, it was done from Norman's memory, drawn from Norman's heart, with purpose other than work. But the greater gift, perhaps, was the thoughtfulness and caring that motivated Norman to create what he did for our grieving family - an expression of his own wordless grief for the loss of a young boy he had known and cared so much about.

I recently asked my uncle, now ninety-two years old, why he thought Norman drew the portrait, and why he thought Norman felt the need to bring it to him personally.

Bob paused, thought a moment, and smiling, he said, "That's just the way he was."

Friday, December 5th

Ken, a UVM classmate of mine, was getting married down in Pawtucket, Rhode Island, and I was an usher in the wedding. After morning chores I drove the two hundred miles to Rhode Island, arriving in plenty of time to try on my tuxedo and get to the wedding rehearsal. It was odd going to my friend's wedding in some way. I had always thought that I would be one of the first to get married. I had a steady girlfriend, but she was still in school and the distance had put a strain on our relationship. She did not go with me to the wedding.

The rehearsal went off without a hitch. All of the bridesmaids and ushers were laughing and joking, and getting to know one another. Like many weddings, the guys knew the guys and the girls knew the girls. By the end of the evening, though, the lines of familiarity were less drawn, and it was just one big group of young people having a good time.

It was hard not to notice the bride's pretty sister, who was the Maid of Honor. She had the bluest eyes I'd ever seen, and a smile that lit up the entire room. She was quick with her words, too, not letting the guys get away with anything. She didn't pay much attention to me, although once in a while I saw her glancing my way. She definitely was not a farm girl, but she wasn't stuck up like some city girls I had met at UVM, either. I thought she was just a fine young woman all the way around.

The wedding day was sunny and cold, and the ceremony went perfectly. The reception was a fun time, too, and everyone started to let loose a bit. I walked over to Louise, the bride, who happened to be standing next to Dot, her Maid of Honor.

"Ken's a lucky fellow," I said, smiling at Louise. "I'm sure you two will be very happy."

"Thank you, Buddy" she replied smiling, "we're really glad you're here. Dot is too, I think," she continued, as she turned and looked at her blushing Maid of Honor.

"On that note, I'm going to go get something to drink," said Dot, embarrassed and joking. "Thanks a lot, Louise," she whispered under her breath at her sister, shaking her head and giggling as she turned to walk away.

"I'll come with you," I said, somewhat startled at how quickly the words had flown out of my mouth. I had seen the two of them talking and had purposely come up with an excuse to walk over and talk to Louise just to start a conversation with Dot, so I was reluctant to have the time be so short.

The two of us fell into step as we went to the punch bowl, then sat down at the head table. I found it remarkably easy to talk with Dot. She was both fun and funny, and I enjoyed making her laugh with stories about farm life. The more she laughed, the more I talked. I'd never been shy or had a problem with the ladies – quite the contrary, I'm almost embarrassed to say – but Dot was different. I wondered what she thought of me. I wondered if she were having as nice a time as I was. I didn't have to wait long to find out.

"Well, nice talking to you, Buddy, maybe we'll meet up at another wedding sometime," she said, warmly, "since I don't see myself being on a Vermont farm anytime soon." Smiling, she got up and went over to another group of people and continued to laugh and joke with them like she had with me.

"It's probably for the best," I thought. "I've already got a serious girl." But thoughts of Dot and those beautiful blue eyes stuck in my mind for months to come.

Christmas

Tommy had not liked Princeton and had developed an ulcer while there, so he left the university and came back to the farm and worked with my dad and me for a bit until changing his school choice to Bard College in Red Hook, New York. It was good to have him home, and he quickly got on his feet. In the tangled complication that his family life had become, it was all the more important for him to be with my folks.

Christmas was quiet. Without small children, it wasn't quite the same, although we still got together with the Rockwells on Christmas Day. Jerry was still overseas, but Peter was back for Christmas Break, and so we spent some time together, catching up and having fun.

Tommy reflected back on those times recently, saying, "Clara was wonderful – very welcoming. What I remember is how warm she was. Nice to us kids, she treated us just like one of her own kids. She was always happy to see you. Jim was a lot of fun, lively. He was always kidding. They were very warm, just marvelous people, you just liked to be around them, they were fun. The Edgertons were extended family, it made a big difference with them next door."

1953

Winter

Mary had been driving back and forth to Stockbridge from West

Arlington for her depression treatments and the drive was getting to be too much for her. It seemed only logical that she would take a small place in Stockbridge where she could spend the night or stay for a few days, so she took a room at a boarding house near the Riggs Center where she was getting her treatment.

Norman, as always, turned to his work during this difficult time. He had gotten it in his head to create an illustration called "The United Nations." He arranged to go to the U.N. with Gene Pelham and photograph Henry Cabot Lodge and ambassadors of other countries. When he got home, he was not satisfied with the result and scrapped the idea. Nothing was working. Nothing was going according to plan. His precious wife was struggling, his sons were gone. Life just wasn't the same – except each morning, as he sat at his studio, here came my dad, like clockwork.

"Mornin' Norman! Whatcha workin' on today?" my father would ask, smiling.

"Come on in and take a look," Norman would say, reaching for his Coke and smoking his pipe.

The two unlikely friends, Norman and Jim, would talk about the weather, the farm, the illustrations, my dad still kidding Norman about running around in chicken dung or being fired from his air raid warden service.

"You know, Norman," my dad said, laughing "I still have the Assistant Air Raid Warden hat hanging in my barn if you want another go at it."

And so for those few moments in the morning, life for Norman was the same, and all was ok.

August

My UVM girlfriend and I had broken up earlier in the summer. The difference in our life goals and the distance between us was just too much. It had been a tough call, but we both knew it was right. I had spent the summer licking my wounds a bit, focusing on the farm and getting things going. Working in the barn, in the fields, and even late at night, I found myself thinking of a beautiful smile and a bubbling personality. Each time I saw Dot's face, I pushed it away. Dot was a city girl, and she had made it clear she was not interested in a farm boy. But when all of my efforts failed to get her out of my mind, I finally sat down and wrote to Ken, my former college roommate - and now her brother-in-law - and asked if he knew whether (a) Dot had a steady boyfriend or not; and (b) if he would subtly try to find out if she might be open to my contacting her.

It didn't take long for Ken to write back. His letter lifted my spirits – Dot was unattached and – the best part - was looking forward to hearing from me! Ken had included her address and phone number so I could get in touch directly. I sat down and wrote in my best handwriting, politely asking if she would like to see a Vermont farm firsthand? I suggested she come during the fall foliage, figuring if nothing else, the beauty of our town would be enough to give her a favorable impression.

Dot wrote back she would be happy to visit in October, and I immediately made the arrangements to have her take a train to Springfield, then a bus to Brattleboro, where I would pick her up.

Things were definitely looking up!

September

Norman often had many models pose for his illustrations before deciding on just the right person to actually use in the final painting. In addition to "The Babysitter," Ardis posed and was not used for "Girl At Mirror," another Rockwell favorite. It shows a young girl sitting on a stool in front of a mirror with a glamour magazine in her lap, leaning on her two hands and thinking. Mary Whalen, a model Norman liked and used a lot, ended up being the model for the young girl. Ardis also posed for "Outside the Principal's Office," the illustration showing a grinning girl with a black eye sitting outside the principal's office. And Mary Whalen ended up being used for the little girl in that illustration, too, although Norman used the black eye from another young girl who had really gotten a shiner.

Ardis was pretty philosophical about Mary being chosen three times over her, even if she was a bit disappointed.

"Either way, whether he used us or not, when you modeled you got your five dollars," said Ardis recently. "Besides, even though Mary was one of his favorite models," she said, her eyes twinkling with laughter, "*I* was always his favorite skating partner."

Friday, October 2nd

My father picked up the slack for the afternoon farm chores so that I could stop and shower. Dot was arriving in Brattleboro in the late afternoon and it would take almost two hours to drive the sixty or so miles to the bus station. I was nervous, excited, happy, scared, all rolled up into one. We had been writing pretty regularly since I first had contacted her in August, and it seemed almost impossible that in a few hours' time she would actually be at our house for the weekend.

I came downstairs and went to my mother in the kitchen. When she saw me, she smiled with approval.

"Go get your girl, you don't want to be late" she said, smiling, waving her hands in the air, shooing me out the door.

"She's just a friend, she's not my girl," I said, embarrassed, but smiling, as I walked over and kissed my mother good-bye on the cheek.

"Not yet," my mother replied, looking up at me and smiling back knowingly, then turned me around toward the door, giving me a playful push, "not yet."

Late October

I walked into the house to have dinner and was surprised to see Norman sitting at our kitchen table. My mom sat across from him with her head down and my dad was standing, leaning against the kitchen sink. It was clear my mom had been crying, something that I had only seen a few times in my life. The last time she had cried had been when Jon passed. My heart started to pound, wondering what tragedy I was going to hear about this time.

My mother started to open her mouth to speak, but no words came out. My dad was looking down at the floor, absently inspecting the fingernails on his right hand. I turned my head and looked at Norman and was surprised to see his eyes were a little teary, too.

"Well, Buddy, I was just talking to your folks here and telling them that, uh, it looks like, well...." and his voice drifted off as he, too, looked down at the table. I turned to my dad questioningly.

My dad took a deep breath and looked me straight in the eye. "Norman is getting a place in Stockbridge so he can be closer to Mary."

I nodded. It made sense Norman might want to have a place in Stockbridge in addition to West Arlington, and we would miss Norman being next door all the time – especially my dad, in the mornings – but, there had been other times Norman and Mary had been gone traveling for extended lengths of time, so I was confused at how upset everyone was at the thought of a temporary separation. Everyone was watching me for my reaction, and seeing the blank look on my face, Norman spoke.

"We're leaving West Arlington for good, Buddy. Selling the place." He paused for a moment, then continued, "We're *moving* to Stockbridge, Buddy..." his voice trailing off, ending in barely a whisper.

My mom pushed back her chair quickly and, pressing her hand to her mouth, ran out of the room and up the stairs. My dad turned around and looked out the window, his back to Norman and me.

"A man's got to think of his family, first, Norman. We do understand...it's just...well...we'll miss you like the dickens, that's all," my dad said, his voice cracking. Without turning back around, he went out the kitchen door and headed toward the barn.

I just stood there, trying to take in the words. It seemed impossible to me that the Rockwells wouldn't be our neighbors anymore. West Arlington without Norman and Mary and the guys wouldn't be right. True, we were all adults now, and I knew logically that the Rockwell boys and the Edgerton kids would have their own lives, perhaps even move away. But it had never occurred to me that Norman wouldn't be in his studio each day; that any other family would ever live in that house. That was the *Rockwell's* house. My mind started to race, like watching a movie in fast motion, so many memories with Tommy and the Rockwells: My first modeling job for Norman; building the studio; playing baseball with Tommy; Edgewell Pond; the basketball hoops in the barn; going to Boston; listening to the Dodgers' games; dragging the deer out of the woods; laughter, so much laughter; the swimming hole; Deer Camp; sugaring; getting Cokes from the studio sink; the scent of Norman's pipe. The truth of it is, I believe that the Edgertons and Rockwells were thrust together as neighbors for a purpose; and it was a wonderful gift that I knew I would always cherish.

As my mind slowly started to take in the words, another horrible thought hit me. If Norman were moving to Stockbridge for good, then it must be because he didn't believe Mary would ever get better. To have made this decision, he must have believed that she would need to be near and/or in the clinic forever. That hit me like a second punch to the stomach. Mary, who had been so instrumental in my life, always so loving and supportive; my mother's best friend; a second mother to my sisters. I reached for the kitchen chair next to Norman and pulled it from the table, scraping the floor, and sat down hard. Norman reached over and clapped his hand on my shoulder. He reached in his pocket and pulled out his pipe and lit it. I was looking down at the table, but could feel him watching me.

"You know, Buddy," he started, "it's not that I want to sell the place, you know that, right? I never intended to leave here, you know that, too, right?"

"Sure, Norman, I understand," I squeaked out, still looking down, my eyes filling up.

"As a matter of fact, I want to show you something, something that was very important to me, that I think says it all."

Norman reached in his pocket and pulled out a piece of paper, folded in squares, and handed it to me. As I opened it up, he said,

"I bought a cemetery plot here in West Arlington. I made sure it was right next to your dad's – we were neighbors in life, and I wanted to be neighbors in death. I always wanted to be by your dad's side, son," he said, his voice cracking. Then, he chuckled, "except the plot wasn't exactly by his *side*, that one was already bought for your mother. I chose the plot at his feet, so I could always reach up and tickle his feet after we both crossed."

I couldn't help but smile at the thought of Norman reaching up and tickling my dad's feet. I wiped away the few tears that had somehow landed on my cheeks. Norman took a big draw on his pipe and continued.

"I want you to have my cemetery plot, Buddy. It's all paid for, and staked out, there are four stone markers with 'R' on them that will show you where it is...guess you'll be wanting to change them to have an 'E' for Edgerton," he said.

"Not on your life, Norman. The 'R' will do me just fine," I said, shaking my head and smiling.

Norman looked down and smiled, before taking a big breath, then looked up at me, his eyes watery.

"You're a fine young man, Buddy Edgerton. A fine young man. It's been a real pleasure to have you in my life and my sons' lives.

And don't you worry – we may be in Stockbridge, but we'll come home to West Arlington to visit. Part of us will *always* be here."

I couldn't reply, just nodded my head and looked down. I heard Norman's chair scrape against the floor as he pushed it back to stand.

"Take care of your mother. She's a good woman," he said, and then he turned and walked out the kitchen door as I laid my head down on the kitchen table and silently cried.

November

In late morning, the Rockwell house was busy with strangers packing and loading the Rockwell possessions onto a moving truck that stood in the driveway between our houses. My dad had taken the cows up the pasture that morning and, oddly, I had not seen him since. Mom was in the kitchen baking pies to send to Stockbridge with Norman. I took a break and, out of habit, headed over to Norman's studio.

"Buddy, come in!" said Norman, as he sat at his easel. Gene Pelham was sitting on the bench beneath the large windows. "I was just going to come over and see if you had a few minutes."

"Sure, Norman, what do you need?" I asked.

"Well, I was hoping you wouldn't mind letting Gene take a few shots of you for me, I'm still trying to figure out what to do with 'The United Nations,' and I'd like you to model for me, if you have a few minutes."

"Sure, Norman," I replied, smiling.

Norman clapped his hands once and jumped up out of his chair, then proceeded to show me what he wanted. He handed me a soldier's helmet and uniform. I changed and came into the studio. Norman had me pose as Gene Pelham clicked away. Modeling for this illustration was the quickest I ever did – just five minutes, and Norman was satisfied with the result.

When we were done, I asked, "Norman, what do you want me to do with the G.I. helmet and uniform?"

"Keep it!" he said, smiling. To this day, I still have the helmet, though the uniform is long since gone, worn out from wearing it while working on the farm.

Norman walked with me to the door and handed me the familiar white envelope with five dollars cash inside.

Looking down and half raising my hand good-bye, I quickly left the studio, not wanting to get emotional, even though it was hard to leave him. As I walked across their backyard toward our house, I noticed Tommy's .22 caliber rifle leaning against a Black Locust tree. It was rusty from sitting outside. I picked it up and headed back to the studio.

"Norman?" I said, "how about if I give Tommy's rifle a good cleaning?"

"Sounds great, Buddy," Norman replied, "and then – keep it. It's yours."

I stood there a moment, not sure what to say, and full of emotion, though I did manage to choke my thanks out to him. Norman, seeing I was upset, came toward me, smiling.

"My first model in this studio, and my last. Somehow, that seems just right."

I stuck out my right hand and as he took it, he pulled me toward him and gave me an uncharacteristic hug.

"Good-bye, Buddy. See you soon. *Soon*."

I nodded my head and smiled, but was unable to reply as I walked out the door. I waved over my shoulder and headed toward the barn.

"Not soon enough," I thought sadly.

*My best wishes and love
to
Clara and Jim Edgerton
My good friend and one-
time neighbors
in good ole Arlington,
Cordially
Norman
Rockwell*

Book signature from Norman to my father and mother in memory of their Arlington years.

CHAPTER NINE
WEST ARLINGTON, VERMONT
1954 - 1959

1954

Saturday, February 13th

After Dot's weekend visit in October, we had written letters regularly and quickly became "an item." She had a way, in her heavy Rhode Island accent, of saying my name that made me grin. I enjoyed telling her stories and making her laugh. We always had a good time whenever we could be together, and we tried to plan trips as often as possible to see one another.

Each year, UVM had a special Winter Carnival around Valentine's Day, called "Kakewalk." In addition to the students, it was traditional for alumni to also come to the campus and enjoy the fun. I invited Dot to come to the carnival with me so that I could show her around my alma mater and introduce her to my fraternity brothers. Many of them would be returning for the winter fun.

We were in downtown Burlington and I was showing her where

I used to hang out when I was in school. I was also giving her a sort of oral history of the town. As we slowly walked, my arm around her shoulders, I suggested we stop for a cup of coffee. It was cold and clear, a beautiful winter day, and the warm coffee would just hit the spot. We went into a small diner and the waitress quickly came over and filled our cups. I sat there, watching Dot drinking her coffee, and my mind began to wander a bit.

"What?" Dot said.

"What do you mean, 'what?'" I replied, startled from my thoughts.

"What are you thinking so hard about?" she asked. She had a way of almost reading my mind.

"Well..." I started, then stopped.

"Buddy, what's wrong?" she said, suddenly looking worried.

"Nothing's wrong at all, it's just that..." I looked away again, trying to find the words.

"Buddy, you're scaring me, will you please just tell me what's going on?" she said, trying to keep her voice steady.

"Well, it's like this," I said matter-of-factly, spreading my hands on the table, "I think that things are going real good, so - let's make it official."

Dot blinked a minute, and then she looked at me kind of puzzled.

"What are you saying, Buddy?" she said, softly.

"I'm saying, I don't know much about diamond rings, but let's go find the biggest one I can afford," I replied, smiling and looking at her over the top of my coffee cup and taking another sip.

Dot opened her mouth and nothing came out, but her eyes were twinkling as she started to grin. She tried again.

"Well, don't just sit there drinking your coffee," she said happily, as she stood up and began gathering her coat and purse "let's go find that diamond ring!"

I stood up, too, and we walked out the door, her hand in the crook of my arm. She leaned against me as we walked from the diner, and we went a few stores down to the jeweler, where we did, indeed, buy the largest ring I could afford with the stash of cash I had had hidden deep in my pants pocket.

The same ring is on her hand today, fifty-five years later. I guess she thought it was going real good, too.

Saturday, July 10th

The day was sunny and cool for summertime in Vermont. The first crop of hay was in and I could afford to be away from the farm for a few days, so Dot and I had picked this day to get married. We had a simple ceremony in Pawtucket, Rhode Island, with family and friends. After the ceremony, we had punch and cake in the church parlor. None of the Rockwells were able to make it, but we heard from them all. For our honeymoon, we went to Boston, then we circled to Howe Caverns and Lake George, New York, and ended up back at the farm in time to take care of the second crop of hay.

The Saturday after we arrived back in Vermont, we had another reception at the Grange Hall in West Arlington to celebrate our marriage. Dot wore her wedding dress and we had another wedding cake. The West Arlington reception had twice as many folks as we had had in Pawtucket, we had a lot of family and friends in Vermont who wanted to celebrate our marriage.

My mother and father gave us an acre of the family land so that we could build our own home. We hadn't finished the house by the time we got married, but it was livable. It had a stove, refrigerator, and a working toilet, but that was about it. Norman and Mary had offered Dot and me their small cottage - Norman even called it the "honeymoon cottage" - which we really appreciated, but since ours was almost finished, we thanked them and stayed at our own place. Dot did a fine job of fixing it up and she quickly learned how to be the wife of a farmer. Life was good.

A few weeks after we returned from our honeymoon, Mary made a trip to West Arlington. She went to my folks' house and my dad called to let us know she was there. Dot and I walked over to the house to see her. I hadn't seen Mary in two years, and when I looked at her for the first time, I was struck by how much she had aged during that time. But when she saw me walk in the door, her face lit up and she rushed over and gave me a big hug. It was so great to see her. She stepped back and looked up at me, smiling, then turned to Dot and hugged her warmly, too.

My mom, dad, Mary, Dot, and I sat altogether in the parlor. Mary had driven to West Arlington to bring Dot and me a wedding present, a lovely pine serving tray. She and Norman also put fifty dollars cash in the wedding card. Fifty dollars in those days was a fortune! We were stunned. We used the money to buy a beautiful coffee table that we still have to this day. For several hours, all of us sat and talked about West Arlington, catching Mary up on local news and reminiscing about the years we had shared as neighbors. Everyone had a good time, but it started getting late, and Mary had to drive back to Stockbridge.

"It was wonderful to see you again, Buddy," Mary said as I walked next to her toward her car. My parents and Dot were a few steps behind. "Your bride is lovely, and you look so happy. I'm glad. I always knew you'd be a good husband one day."

"Well, Dot makes it easy," I said, smiling, "she's the best. I've always been lucky to have special folks come into my life. Like you and Norman - no matter where you are, you're always here, too." I held my arms out toward the two yards. I had to say it, even if it was difficult, because it was true. I wanted Mary to know that it didn't matter that they were in Stockbridge, and that we didn't think it was her fault that they had had to move. Family was family, by blood or by heart, and the Rockwells were family by heart, pure and simple.

Mary just smiled, and her eyes were a bit watery as she hugged us each good-bye. She held onto my mom and dad a long time before climbing into her car.

"I'll come see you again, soon," she promised, smiling through her tears and waving out the car window at all of us as she drove down the driveway toward the covered bridge.

"Soon!" my mom shouted, waving and holding back tears, "come back soon, Mary! We miss you!"

I stood next to Dot with my arm around her shoulders, not knowing I was waving good-bye to Mary for the last time.

Saturday, September 25th

As the months and years went by, we stayed in touch with the

Rockwells through letters and occasional phone calls. Long distance was very expensive then, but Mary would ring my mother once in a while. Norman had settled into life in Stockbridge. He was still illustrating covers for the Saturday Evening Post, and we enjoyed buying any copy of the Post that had been done by Norman.

Through the window over the kitchen sink, Dot and I saw my mom coming toward our house mid-afternoon, smiling, a magazine rolled up under her right arm. I met her at the front door.

"Take a look at this!" she said, smiling, as she came into the house, and handed me the latest Saturday Evening Post.

On the cover sat a farm boy on the running board of an old familiar farm truck. He was dressed in an ill-fitting suit and was sitting next to a man who clearly was his father, a farmer with well-worn hands. A dog sadly rested its head on the leg of the boy. A suitcase with a "State U" sticker on its side rested at the young man's feet; a package of food was in the boy's hands.

"Remind you of anyone?" my mom asked.

"Just a little bit," I said, grinning, "just a little bit."

The cover, *Breaking Home Ties*, is one of Norman's most loved illustrations. Like I said before, I am sure that this was inspired by my going off to the University of Vermont and how that impacted my dad and the farm; but, as importantly for me, my going off to school had grown from my relationship with Norman and Mary. Without their support (and borderline insistence) I never would have gone to college and never would have had the life I have lived.

The ties of true friendship – regardless of time and distance - can never be broken.

Fall

Dot and I had been married about three months when the leaves started changing in the Valley. My chicken venture was continuing, but not as successfully as I would have liked, so I was thinking about stopping that part of the farm business in the Spring. The farm was not really big enough for two families to live from, and Dot and I spent a lot of time talking about our future and what it would look like.

"Buddy," Dot said one night, her back to me as she prepared supper, "we need to be thinking long term – especially now."

"Why now, Dot? I'm always thinking long term, but why do you say that?" I asked.

Dot turned around, smiling.

"Because soon there will be three of us to think about, not just you and me."

It took a minute for the meaning of her words to sink in.

"A BABY?" I asked, excitedly.

"Well, I'm not talking about a cow!" said Dot, laughing. "Seriously, yes, Buddy, a baby. We're going to have a baby."

"Well, I'll be. I'm going to be a father!" I said, proudly. "Me! *A father!*" I finally found my feet and jumped up, grabbed Dot around the waist, and whirled her around the room, laughing.

"Buddy?" Dot said suddenly, not laughing at all.

"What, dear?" I replied, wanting to do anything, everything, for my wife and my baby-to-be.

"Please stop the whirling – I'm going to throw up," she said, rushing to the bathroom.

1955

January

I had prepared a business plan for the farm and the end result was obvious. We had expanded our herd as much as was possible, given the land we had, and still the income from the farm was not enough to support two families. With my father's blessing, I left the farm and took a job with the University of Vermont. It was a special two-year project funded by the University, and I was designated a Farm and Home Business Counselor. Dot and I moved to Montpelier and rented a small apartment. My job took me throughout the state and I was gone quite a bit. During that time, Dot was frequently alone and without family support, which wasn't easy. But, Dot knew I enjoyed the work making a difference in farm family's lives, and Dot - being Dot - made it easy on me. She was certainly the best part of *my* long-term planning!

March

"Greetings!" said the beginning of the letter in my hand. Leaving the farm meant my farm deferment from the draft was no longer valid. Even though I had a medical condition that should have precluded me from the service, Uncle Sam saw fit to order me to report for duty in the U.S. Army in April. With Dot's due date of mid-May, I requested – and received – a deferment until July 3rd, just one week before Dot's and my first anniversary.

"We'll have other anniversaries to celebrate," Dot said good-naturedly. "I'm not going anywhere - even if *you* apparently are going to Fort Dix, New Jersey!"

Thursday, May 12th

It was unseasonably warm for May in Vermont the day our son, James Albert Edgerton, Jr., came into this world. He was the most beautiful baby I had ever seen. I couldn't get enough of watching him, and the feeling that filled my chest each time I held him can't be put into words.

Beyond my love and pride for our son, I understood many things about the world differently after he was born. I understood what had kept my father going when all else around him had failed – losing his herd twice; losing his son. I understood what had kept my mother going when she was tired and heavy with another child. I understood what kept Norman at the easel each and everyday, from early in the morning until late in the night. I understood what motivated Mary to want to get well. I was even more amazed at the trust that Norman and Mary had shown when they had let me take Tommy to New York, alone. I understood in a different way what being a good son had meant, to my parents, and in a very real way, to Norman and Mary, too.

I understood what it was to be a man.

Saturday, June 25th

I loaded up the farm truck with the crib, playpen, and other baby items, plus several suitcases for Dot and Jim, and drove them down to Dot's mother's house. While in the service I would receive thirty-six dollars

247

per month for expenses and Dot would receive a whopping seventy-six dollars a month for her and Jim. It only made sense that she would move in with her mother to help stretch the scarce dollars for their care.

I spent the night with them and then was going to head back to West Arlington the next day. That week, I had to finish up my work obligations in preparation for my induction into the Army over the Fourth of July weekend. I was to report by 6:00 p.m. on July 3rd for basic training at Fort Dix, New Jersey. My folks would take me to town early in the day, where an Army bus would pick me up along Route 7. There would be many stops along the way in small towns all over New England as the Army gathered its new troops.

When it was time to leave Dot, she and I walked outside to the truck. Jim was sound asleep in Dot's arms, totally unaware of everything except being fed and safe. I looked down at my bride and my son and suddenly I felt a little shaky. I had no problem fighting for my country, but the good-bye was more difficult than I had expected. Dot looked up and, already knowing me so well, took charge.

"Now Buddy, you get in that truck and go make me proud. Whatever we have to deal with, we'll deal with it," she said firmly.

"Piece of cake," I replied, smiling down at her.

"And when you come home on leave, a piece of *anniversary* cake – I still have the top of our wedding cake in the freezer. Now doesn't *that* sound good!" she said, laughing and shooing me into the truck before both of us fell apart.

Saturday, December 24th

Christmas came early in West Arlington. I had completed my basic training in Fort Dix and had had my leave, then had headed back to Fort Dix for my next assignment, an administrative position also at Fort Dix. I had a severe form of arthritis that had worsened while in service and much of the time after my basic training I was in a base hospital. The decision was finally made by the military powers that be that I was not physically fit for service and I received a medical discharge on Christmas Eve. I had served five months and nineteen days.

It was late evening when a taxi dropped me off at 103 Morris Avenue, Pawtucket. The sky was clear, but the temperature was well below zero. As I climbed out of the car, I enjoyed the smell of the night air. It felt good to be with family again.

As I started to walk across the street toward Dot's mother's house, I saw a petite figure standing at the door, waving. She held a package in her arms. As I came toward her, I saw that the "package" was my now seven-month old son, who was smiling and wriggling in Dot's arms, anxious to get down and on the move.

"The best Christmas present ever!" I thought, looking down at my family.

"Welcome home!" Dot said quietly through her tears, "welcome home!"

1956

Spring

Mary called my mom, as she did on occasion, and shared frightening news with us. Peter, now twenty years old and at Haverford College, had had a fencing accident at school and had nearly died. The point of the opponent's blade had barely missed the main artery of his heart. My mother, though shaken by the news, kept her composure and talked with Mary a long time, calming her down. My mother had a way of helping Mary, using her quiet strength to help bring Mary back into balance. This was a part of their strong friendship, woman-to-woman, and by the time they were done talking, Mary felt better.

It was only after she hung up that my mother took a deep breath and allowed herself room to be upset, too.

July

My two-year job in Montpelier lasted only one year. At the end of the first year I had prepared a written report that showed we had finished the project. On June fifteenth, I was hired by UVM to work as the 4-H County Agent in the UVM County Extension office in Bennington, Vermont, about twenty miles from West Arlington – considerably better than working in Montpelier.

When I wasn't working at my job, I was working on our house. Dot and I finished the inside and outside ourselves, making it bigger, and gradually turning it into a home. I also helped my dad out on the farm when he needed me, especially during haying season or sugaring season when one pair of hands was not enough. We had a deal. He loaned me money to help pay for building my house, and I worked the loans off on the farm, at a rate of two dollars per hour. Dot and I also got our milk from the farm, as well as fruits and vegetables.

Life was simple, and everyone was healthy. There were no hurricanes, floods, diseases, illnesses, deaths, or losses, no big changes. The pains of our distant past almost seemed not real. There was a rhythm to our lives, different than the rhythm of the farm I had known growing up, but as comforting. I was grateful for the regularity and routine.

"It's nice to be settled, isn't it, Dot?" I asked. "We have a good life. No surprises. We know what to expect. Don't you agree?"

"Um, well, sort of," Dot said.

"What do you mean?" I asked.

"Well, about that regularity, routine, and no surprises part…"

"Yes, Dot?"

"Well, uh…*surprise!*" she said smiling and throwing her hands up in the air and waving them, "I'm pregnant, again."

Seven months later, on February 20, 1957, our beautiful daughter, Deborah Joy, arrived.

Thursday, July 25th

If you think about it, the passing of a family member or friend is like a milestone in our lives. It creates a before/after understanding in our awareness, a kind of "they were there/they weren't there" marker that affects our memories and, in some way, defines the memories. And even if you know that your elderly loved ones grow closer to death, the reality still comes as a bit of a shock.

My Grandma Edgerton, who had lived in our farmhouse from the time she was six months old to the day she died, including living with my parents their entire married life, slipped away quietly in the morning. She had outlived her husband by twenty years and had witnessed three wars (WWI, WWII and Korea), the Industrial Revolution, the Wall Street Crash of 1929, the Depression, air flight, the telephone, and had she lived three more months, she would have witnessed Sputnik I going into orbit. In all those years, her expression barely changed, which made her the perfect inspiration and model for Norman in "Going and Coming."

She wasn't a warm, loving type of grandmother, but she was always a part of the important moments in our lives; and she was much missed after she was gone.

1959

Late May

Dot and I were number fourteen on the party line – two long rings followed by four short. One Saturday afternoon in late May, the phone rang and Dot and I stood still, counting. Riiiinnng-riiiiinnng-ring-ring-ring-ring! Ours!

"Hello!" I said cheerily.

"Buddy? This is Norman!"

"Hey Norman! How are you? How's Mary? Is everything ok?" I asked.

"Everything's fine, just fine. Look, I was wondering if you could make it down to Stockbridge next weekend to model for me again. I need a young, handsome fellow like you for a painting for Upjohn. It pays fifty dollars. Thought you and Dot might need a few things for the family, and you're perfect for this job."

This was *great* news, and I eagerly agreed. I was to be a young veterinarian, so I went by Doc Lampear's vet office in Bennington and borrowed a white coat and other vet instruments as props.

The next Saturday, I drove down to Stockbridge to Norman's new studio. It was odd to see him working in a different studio, but the layout reminded me very much of his West Arlington studio. The actual modeling process was pretty much the same, but this time Norman had me sign a model's release form, which was the first time I had had to do that.

"Lawyers." said Norman shrugging, "My business manager says we have to do this now. Seems kinda sad we have to live in the kind of world where a handshake isn't enough."

"It's not like it used to be," I said, nodding my head, "but I'm happy to do it."

Mary was no where to be seen, and Norman didn't volunteer much information, other than to say she was "getting better." We didn't chat long because I had a long drive home, but when I left we shared a big bear hug.

"Come down sometime when you can visit longer, Buddy, and bring your folks. Would love to see them," Norman said as he walked me to the door.

"Soon, Norman, we'll have to do that soon," I said.

Tuesday, August 25th

My modeling job for Norman could not have come at a better time. I had decided to go back to school part-time to get my Master's Degree and that summer I was attending George Washington

University to take six credits in Human Development toward my degree. I was in school from June 15th through August 1st and then returned home to West Arlington. Dot had taken Jim and Deb, now four and two years old, to visit with her family in Rhode Island while I was in D.C.

We all came home to West Arlington the end of the first week in August. My parents had planned a vacation down at Cape Cod with the Wilcoxes for the last week of the month and I had assured my dad I would be home in time to tend to the farm chores while they were gone.

Their big day came and they drove off happily, my folks had never taken a vacation before. I waved at them as they headed over the covered bridge and for the next few days I was back in the rhythm of farming our land.

I came to the house after finishing the night milking when I heard the phone start ringing. I automatically started counting the rings and realized it was a call for my parents' house. It occurred to me it was probably my father or mother, calling to make sure everything was ok.

"Jim?" said a familiar male voice.

"No, this is Buddy, my folks are out of town – *Tommy?*" I asked.

"Yeah, Buddy, it's Tommy…" his voice trailed off.

"Tommy, what's wrong?" I asked, feeling my stomach start to tie up in knots.

"It's my mom, Buddy. She had a heart attack earlier this afternoon, and - she's gone, Buddy, she's gone," he said quietly.

I was stunned. Mary was only fifty-one years old. We

knew she had had her problems, but dying of a heart attack was a total shock. I pulled myself together and tried to put myself in Tommy's position.

"What can I do, Tommy?" I asked gently.

"If you'd tell your folks for me, I'd appreciate it. I'll be in touch with the funeral details when I know them. I've gotta go. Good to hear your voice, Buddy," he said.

"You, too, Tommy. We'll be thinking of you," I said, as he hung up the phone.

I stood there, stunned, with the phone in my hand. Norman without Mary was unthinkable. The world without Mary was unthinkable. I was suddenly flooded with memories, from the first moment she had introduced herself and the boys to me, up until the last time I had seen her, when she brought Dot and me our wedding present. Mary laughing; Mary reading; Mary helping get models for Norman; Mary signing my school bus petition; Mary at the Swimming Hole; Mary hugging me good-bye for the last time.

My mom and dad had left a phone number for emergencies and I slowly dialed the number. My father had answered the phone cautiously, knowing that my calling them while on vacation wouldn't be for a happy reason. When I told him Mary had passed, there was only a long silence on the other end of the phone. I even thought he might have hung up. Finally, I heard my father let out a big sigh.

"I'll talk to your mother and we'll give you a call back and let you know when we'll be home," he said, his voice cracking. "And Buddy, if you talk to Tommy again – send our love."

He hung up the phone abruptly, before I could say anything. It was a day where saying nothing was the only thing that felt right.

A few days later, services were held for Mary in Stockbridge. My folks had made it home in time to get there and I had stayed at the farm to do the chores so that my dad could go. I would have liked to have been there for all of the Rockwells, especially Tommy, but I understood that my mom and dad needed to attend.

The morning of the funeral, I was thinking about Norman and Mary as I led the cows past the million dollar incinerator and up the back pasture. I still couldn't believe Mary was gone, perhaps because thoughts and memories of her were still so strong. To this day, I still can hear her: "Just do the right thing, Buddy."

She was a very gentle, very *special* lady, Mary Rockwell. After all these years, I still miss her.

CHAPTER TEN
WEST ARLINGTON, VERMONT
1960 - 1978

1960

Saturday, February 13th

Six years to the day since I proposed to Dot, the first excerpts of Norman's autobiography, "Norman Rockwell: My Adventures As An Illustrator" appeared in the Saturday Evening Post. The cover of that issue is one of Norman's most famous, the "Triple Self-Portrait." Tommy had collaborated with Norman on the book and it was an instant success.

The book was fascinating, entertaining, and full of rich detail, covering all the way up to a few days before Mary died. While the last chapter of the book chronicles Norman's struggle with illustrating "The Family Tree" day-by-day from April 27, 1959 through August 19th, six days before Mary died. The book ends on an "up" note, and there isn't even a hint of her passing, other than the dedication in the hardcover edition which reads, "To Mary,

Whose loving help has meant so much to me."

Knowing Norman, it makes some kind of sense that he would have written the book so soon after Mary's death; that he would immerse himself in a big professional undertaking such as his autobiography and the "Triple Self-Portrait." Work was always Norman's antidote.

That's just the way he was.

1961

Fall

It had been more than a year since Mary had passed away unexpectedly and Norman had begun seeing a woman in Stockbridge, Mollie Punderson. Like both of Norman's first two wives, Mollie had also been a schoolteacher. They had met when Norman joined a poetry discussion group that she led. He had joined it to get out of the house and to try to meet new people.

Mollie was a kind woman and Norman had strong feelings for her. It was important to him, however, that his dear friends, my mom and dad, meet Mollie before he went any further in their relationship. He trusted my mom and dad, both in terms of their ability to size up people, and also in their honesty to tell Norman exactly what they thought, if asked.

Norman called my dad and asked if he might bring Mollie by for them to meet, and my dad said it would be fine, of course. One Sunday afternoon in the fall, Norman drove up and introduced her to my folks. Dot, the kids, and I came over to say hello, too.

Mollie was a very nice woman and it was nice to see Norman smiling again. We had heard that he had had a tough time after Mary died, and it was good to see him so happy. They spent the day at my folks' farm. Norman showed Mollie around West Arlington, and when it was time to go, I took several pictures of them all. I think one of the pictures that is the most telling is a photo of my mom and dad with Norman and Mollie. From left to right, they stood: Norman, Mom, Mollie, and then Dad. Norman's arm is around my mom's shoulders, but his hand is lightly touching Mollie's shoulder. Mollie is leaning in toward my dad. All four are smiling. They look like they have been friends for years.

Before leaving to go back to Stockbridge, Norman pulled my mother aside.

"And?" he asked, scared but making himself put the question to my mom.

"And, what?" she asked, a bit confused.

"And...and....and....do you like her?" Norman asked.

"Yes, yes I do," my mother replied, "and what's important is that *you* do, Norman. Mary wanted you to be happy, she told me that many, many times. If this relationship makes you happy, I'm all for it - and I'm sure Mary would be, too."

Norman's face relaxed.

"Jim's a lucky man, Clara," he said, grinning.

"Mollie's lucky too, Norman," she responded with a smile.

Wednesday, October 25th

It was a crisp fall day in Stockbridge when Norman and Mollie made it official. The quiet ceremony marked the beginning of a wonderful marriage between two people who genuinely loved one another through their later years. We were all happy for Norman that he had found yet another lovely woman to share his life.

1964

Spring

I hadn't worked on my Master's degree for five years. I had been busy with my job, finishing our house, supporting my dad with the farm, and spending time with Dot and the kids. There just hadn't been the time or the funds to continue what I had started at George Washington University in 1959.

I was held in high regard at my work with the UVM County Extension Service and as a result I was offered an incredible opportunity. I was given half my salary for one year in order to pursue finishing my Master's Degree in Extension Education at UVM full-time. I began in the Spring and took courses through summer and the fall of 1964, finishing up at Christmas and officially receiving my degree in May of 1965. While I was in school, Dot went back to work as a bank teller. With two school-aged children, it wasn't easy for Dot to work and hold down the home front, but it was worth the sacrifice to further my education.

When I went to the Commencement exercises I felt sure that, along with my wife and parents, somewhere Mary was proud, too.

Fall

In the midst of studying at the kitchen table, the party line rang. Dot and I waited and counted. Yep, it was a call for us.

"Hello!" I said, enjoying a quick break from my schoolwork.

"Buddy? Norman. Listen, I was wondering if you could take a drive down to Stockbridge. Got another modeling job for you, if you're interested."

"Sure, Norman," I said, "when do you need me?"

"Tomorrow, if that's ok. And also, how old is your little Jimmy these days?" he asked.

"He turned nine earlier this year, can you believe it? About the same age Tommy was when you moved next door to us!" I said, shaking my head.

"Well, if you think it would be ok if he missed a day of school, I sure could use him, too. I'm doing another scout calendar, and he's the perfect age for the Cub Scout."

"Will do, Norman, we'll come by late morning," I said.

"Ok, sounds good," Norman replied, "gotta go. Give your mom my best, and your dad and Dot, too, of course. See you tomorrow!"

Before I could say good-bye, I heard the click on the other end of the phone. I could just imagine him already back at work before I had had a chance to sit back down at the kitchen table. That's just the way he was.

The next day, Jimmy and I drove down to Stockbridge. Jim's eyes got wide when he saw a real Coke machine in the corner.

"Would you like to have a Coke, Jimmy?" Norman asked, smiling.

"Boy, would I!" he said, looking at all of the war artifacts and props hanging on the walls and set up around the studio.

The session went fairly quickly. Norman took profile shots of me in different scout uniforms and also took profile shots of Jimmy dressed in a Cub Scout uniform. The illustration, "Growth of a Leader," became the 1966 Scout calendar. In the final version, Norman used me at my real age (thirty-four) for the Scout Leader, aged me ten years for the Scout Master, and took off twenty years for the Boy Scout.

At the end of the session, I signed the new model release forms and Norman handed each of us the familiar white envelope. He had given Jimmy thirty-five dollars and me, fifty dollars.

"Start your college fund," Norman said to Jimmy, patting his head, laughing. "It's important."

Seeing the confusion on Jimmy's face, I said, "And you can pick out a baseball glove, too."

"Thanks, Mr. Rockwell!" Jimmy said, suddenly hugging him around the waist. It was only the second time Norman had seen my son, but the connection was there nonetheless.

Norman got a little teary-eyed as he hugged him back.

"Call me Norman. You're a good boy," he said softly, "just like your Daddy was."

1970

November

My dad's interest in his community, combined with downsizing his farm, led him to want to more actively be a part of the government decisions that affected the State of Vermont. So, in 1970, at the age of sixty-four, my father ran for a State Representative seat and won. He was re-elected in 1972, serving a total of four years.

My dad had always stood up for what he felt was right – going all the way back to his minority opinion on the school construction issue that had inspired Norman's Freedom of Speech – so it didn't really come as a surprise. Still, I was proud that he would take the step of actively representing the people of the State of Vermont in the State Legislature. It was all about doing the right thing, for his family *and* for his fellow man.

That was my dad.

1974

Fall

I surprised my folks with a visit, and it was my turn to be surprised when they told me they were on their way down to Stockbridge to visit Norman and Mollie.

"Wanna come with us, Buddy?" asked my mom.

"Sure, I can do that," I said, "it's been a long time. Would be good to see them."

We arrived shortly before lunch and Mollie answered the door.

"Norman was upstairs, taking a nap," she said. "He'll be down shortly."

She took us into their living room and we all chatted for a few minutes until Norman appeared in the doorway. He had aged considerably since I had seen him during our modeling session for "Growth of a Leader," and I knew my mom was startled, too, though she recovered her composure quickly.

My mother jumped up and hugged him warmly, and Norman's face lit up. He and my dad shook hands firmly, as did he and I. As he made his way to the dining room table, Norman moved slowly and at times seemed a bit confused. Mollie was kind and gentle with him, and we were glad to see he was in good hands.

After chatting about half an hour, I asked Norman if he would mind signing some prints of "County Agent" I had. The illustration Norman had painted almost thirty years before was still one of the most loved and popular images among County Extension Services. I wanted to give an autographed print to five members of my staff who were retiring.

"Sure, Buddy! No problem," Norman said cheerfully.

I went to the trunk of my car and pulled out six prints – five for my staff, one for me. Norman sat at the dining room table and carefully signed each print. When he got to mine, he wrote, "My very best wishes to, Bud Edgerton, my friend. Cordially, Norman Rockwell." We took some pictures with Norman and my mom; Norman and my dad; and Norman and me. We laughed and joked, and then Norman seemed to be tiring, so we knew it was time to go.

As we all walked to the door, I couldn't help but think that when Norman and Mary had moved in next door, he had been almost the exact same age as I was at that point. When I was a kid, he had seemed like such a "grown-up," an adult, my best friend's Dad – and now here I was, married with two children of my own, successful in large part because of the three people who stood smiling and hugging one another good-bye at the door.

Life was funny that way, I suppose. The cycles were there, if you looked for them. The themes of the generations – in some ways, anyway – never changed. It was those moments of life, those threads of understanding that passed from parent to child, that Norman was so talented in capturing in his paintings. It's what made his artwork connect with such a wide range of people, different age levels, different economic levels, the realization that underneath it all, we were all very much alike. Norman understood that about people. He even understood it about himself.

That's just the way he was.

1978

Wednesday, November 8th

The day was overcast and not terribly cold by Vermont standards in November. The morning air was above freezing and in the afternoon it was even close to fifty degrees. I didn't notice anything out of the ordinary that day as I went about my job, but before the day was over I learned something that changed my life forever. Norman had died of emphysema.

The country was saddened by the lost of such a beloved artist. The New York Times obituary read, "Rockwell shared with Walt Disney the extraordinary distinction of being one of the two artists familiar to nearly everyone in the U.S., rich or poor, black or white, museum goer or not, illiterate or Ph.D." It was hard to imagine a life without Norman and his talent.

We all knew it was coming, of course. Norman was eighty-four years old and had been failing for some time. I had talked to Jerry over the years and he quietly had shared with me that at times toward the end of his life, Norman had forgotten how to mix his colors. It broke my heart to hear that; Norman was too vibrant and independent a person to lose his art.

The funeral took place on Saturday, November 11th. My parents went, but I made a decision that even now brings up some conflict in my heart. You see, that Saturday was the first day of deer hunting season. And, when I thought about being at Norman's services, I couldn't face it. I wanted to remember Norman as he had been, I didn't want to have his funeral as the last thoughts of him in my mind. I thought about hunting in West Arlington and the solitude of being on our land, land that was forever tied to the memories of Norman, Mary, and the boys. And I decided it felt more right to go off in the woods with my thoughts of Norman than it was to go to Stockbridge to his funeral.

My parents sat silently with the Rockwell boys at the front of the services; I silently headed up Benedict Hollow to hunt. The minister raised his voice to speak of Norman and his many lifetime achievements – being recognized by the National Chamber of Commerce as "a great living American" in 1957; being the first inductee into The Society of Illustrators' Hall of Fame in 1959; receiving the Presidential Medal of Freedom in 1977, the highest civilian award from the government there is; painting four presidents: Eisenhower, Kennedy, Johnson, and Nixon – as I raised my gun. I could hear my father's voice in my head: "Use your ears! They don't have bells on!" There was a crack of a twig and the buck appeared.

I took aim, and the rifle's blast echoed from ridge-to-ridge. The crowd of people who came to pay their last respects had circled around the Rockwell family. The emptiness of the woods had allowed me to circle around the deer. Tears were shed at the memorial. And tears were shed in the solitude of Benedict Hollow.

I thought of the man, the neighbor, the friend, that was Norman Rockwell as I walked through the trees, leaves scattered like a blanket on the ground, creeping my way to my favorite deer stand on Jim's Ridge. He was closer to me there than he would have been in Stockbridge. My mind began to race as my feet did, navigating through the woodland. It wasn't just the memories of our families' times together, it was how I had looked up to Norman, the greatness of the man. He was never ruined by praise, he would rather be saved by criticism. He never said "I." He was never envious or jealous. He was always a good listener – always. He helped others when he could, but left others' pride intact at the same time. He was loyal to a fault. He contributed to his community. He was a good friend, a good neighbor. He would never intentionally harm anyone or anything. He cared deeply about those he loved, even if sometimes it was hard for him to show it. Quite simply, he was as kind, sincere, and genuine as one could possibly be.

That's just the way he was.

1979

Tuesday, March 19th

Four months after Norman passed, my father died of a heart attack.

He was being treated for prostate cancer, but in the end it was a sudden heart incident that took his life. It was inconceivable to me that the two men I respected and looked up to most in the world were gone. My mother didn't say much, it wasn't her way to show her pain. She was much better at showing her love, warmth, and joy. The pain, well - she had always held that close to her heart.

My sisters and I came together in West Arlington and sat in the funeral parlor as a stream of people came to call. There were many familiar faces, but after a while they all blended together. I focused my attention on making sure my mother and sisters were ok and somehow got through the day.

A few days later we held the funeral. As I stood in the front of the West Arlington Methodist Church about to go inside for the services, I saw a smiling, familiar face moving toward me. It was Tommy. As I started toward Tommy, I realized that Jerry was right behind him. We all broke into a big smile at the sight of one another. I was glad they were there. We embraced warmly and then sat down together, Tommy and Jerry sitting up front with our family, of course. It was only right.

As I listened to the service, I could not help but think about Norman giving me his cemetery plot, and how he had wanted to be buried next to my father so he could tickle my dad's feet. I hoped that somewhere, he was still able to do it.

Somehow, thinking about my father and Norman, two friends still close in death as they had been in life, comforted me in a way that nothing else did.

CHAPTER ELEVEN
SOUTH BURLINGTON, VERMONT
2009

It seems only right to share where things are now, given how much I've told you about how things were along the way. My sister Edith is now eighty years old. She was widowed in 1984 from her husband, Stanley and is currently living in an assisted living home in Manchester. She was married and did not have children, but she worked for many years as a secretary for an insurance agency in Albany, New York.

Joy completed her dental hygienist schooling and ultimately worked as a Dental Health Educator in the public schools after working several years in her profession. She and her husband Bob had a daughter, Karen, and a son, Peter, and after more than fifty years they are still happily married and living in Altamont, New York.

My younger sister Ardis was married and had two sons, Marshall and Miner, and a daughter, Brenda. She was widowed in 1999 from her husband Ray, and now is a proud grandmother of nine (including two sets of twins!) and a great-grandmother of two. She spends her time between Florida and Vermont.

Dot and I had moved to Woodstock in 1966 when I received a promotion to Area Administrator for the University of Vermont, and then to South Burlington in 1977, where we still live to this day. I retired in 1986 after more than thirty successful years with the University of Vermont Extension Service.

Jerry Rockwell is a famous artist in his own right and lives in Massachusetts with his wife, Nova. They have one daughter, Daisy. In 2007, Jerry completed a six-month position as an artist-in-residence in Scottsdale, where he completed a fourteen-foot, thirty-one tiered sculpture, "Maya II."

Tommy and his wife, Gail, have a son, Barnaby, and a daughter, Abigail. Tommy now lives in Poughkeepsie, New York, and is a distinguished author, having published eighteen books to date, primarily for young people. One of his most famous children's books, "How To Eat Fried Worms," was made into a film in 2006. In 1959, he worked with his father to write, "My Adventures As An Illustrator: An Autobiography."

Peter became a famous stone sculptor. He and his wife, Cinny, have lived in Italy since 1961, when they went for a six-month visit and never left. They have four children, Geoffrey, Tom, and twins Mary and John.

My mother outlived the other of the Edgerton-Rockwell "parents" by many years. She became quite debilitated in her old age. Years of hard, physical labor ultimately had taken their toll. She lived alone after my father passed away, until finally my sisters and I had to make the decision to move her into a nursing home facility. It was not an easy decision to move her and let go of the family farm after it had been in our family for so many generations, but there wasn't anyone who was in a position to live there. All of us had moved out of the area and had lives of our own that were far removed from the farmhouse of our youth.

After selling the property, we held an estate sale. As I cleaned out a dresser from my mother's bedroom, I noticed an old magazine in one of the drawers. My mother had become somewhat of a pack rat in her later years, and we had already gotten rid of stacks of magazines and other papers that seemed like trash, so I started to throw this one away, too. As I pulled the magazine out of the drawer, a piece of paper fell out of the center of it. It was the original preview of Norman's "A Guiding Hand," in perfect condition, hidden between the pages of an old edition of Ladies Home Journal. I can't help but wonder if there had been other sketches or previews in the many magazines we had thrown away – Norman had always been generous with my parents - but that's in the past, and there wasn't much else we could have done about it then or now. Kinda makes you think, though.

On Thursday, March 22nd of 2007, the nursing home called to let me know that my ninety-three year old mother had quietly passed away early that morning. In her later years she had been unable to communicate with us, trapped in her mind, but her eyes were still as clear and blue as I remember from when I was a young boy. As she sat silently in her wheelchair, I wondered if she were hunting in the woods with my father or sitting at the Swimming Hole with Mary as all of us kids swung on the rope and dropped into the middle of the Battenkill. When we called her name, perhaps she heard us calling her from across the room at a Grange Hall dance on a summer Saturday night. As I kissed her cheek, maybe she remembered the years I was a boy, still young enough to be willing to reach up and kiss her good-night. I'd like to think so; I'm sure the memories of those times would be a comfort to her beyond anything that the present times could have given her.

After her private services, Dot and I drove to West Arlington. It just felt right to go "home." We crossed the bridge and headed up the small road toward the two houses, ours and the Rockwell's. Dot knew me well enough to sit quietly by my side. We parked along The Green and walked along River Road in front of the houses. The yard in front of my family's house was now full of clover. I couldn't help but feel sad when I saw an electric fence for the horses.

Dot and I walked between the two houses and stood looking at the backyards. It was so different. There was a fence dividing the properties. I couldn't even imagine having a barrier between our two families – growing up, there was never really a "theirs" and "ours," it was more like one big yard between us. In my childhood, there had been small saplings, a pond, a low stone wall, and everything was open. Now, the trees had almost sixty years' growth, and they stood tall and strong, giving shade all the way to the edges of the yards.

Yet, for all of the differences, there was still a sense of familiarity. I was relieved to see that Norman's studio looked the same. The houses still rose up, like white twins. The last sign of a morning mist was clearing off the mountain behind our houses, just like it had so many mornings after chores were done.

I closed my eyes for a few moments, breathing in the smells of my childhood – the pasture, the trees, the mountain air. And as I stood there, alone in my thoughts, I would swear I heard the

272

sounds of our families – my mother calling across the yard to Mary as she and the girls hung the laundry; my father standing at the studio door, "Whatcha workin' on, Norman?" and Norman's reply, "Well, come on in and take a look;" the baseball being thrown back and forth between Tommy and me, making a dull thud as it hit our mitts. There was laughter between the guys, giggling from the girls, and my father's voice, gruffly giving instructions on how to drive the Doodlebug. It was so real, I almost didn't want to come back from my thoughts.

But, time being what it is, it was time to head back to South Burlington. We drove the two and a half hours home in silence. It wasn't the kind of silence where there is anger, it was all the feelings of my thoughts that deserved quiet; a respectful reflection of my mother's life and my youth.

We arrived home in South Burlington in late afternoon as the sun was starting to set. It had snowed a few days before, so we went into the house through the garage, carefully taking off our snow boots and placing them on the shoe tray just inside the door. Inside, the house was quiet except for the sound of a mantle clock ticking in the living room.

The telephone doesn't ring as often in my Vermont home as it used to. Jim and Deb are long since grown, with families of their own. My retirement days are busy with errands and doctor's appointments, trips to the grocery, and yard work that never ends until the snow comes. My wife, Dot, and I have thoroughly enjoyed our fifty-five years together. She's still my gal, even though I don't say it much, and I can still make her blush with just a hint of a private smile.

I suppose it's only natural when you're seventy-nine years old and think back over your life, to ponder at times what it was, what it wasn't, maybe even what it might have been. When I decided to write this book, it brought up a lot of feelings that I had forgotten somewhere along the way, and that was a good thing, one of the best parts about writing this story down.

All in all, if I had to sum it up, I'd say it's pretty simple and it all comes down to this: My life was, literally, like a Norman Rockwell illustration; and it was a much better life because Norman, Mary, Jerry, Tommy, and Peter, were such an important part of it.

That's just the way it was.

Greetings from Mollie and Norman Rockwell

REFLECTIONS
FROM THE CO-AUTHOR

The story of how Bud and I met, how this book came to be written, and the impact it has had on my life, is serendipitous. It seemed only right to share the "story behind the story" with you, now that you have finished reading about Bud's amazing life.

In 2004, I was primarily making my living as a writer in Atlanta. Yet, my entire life I had been intuitive which, while an integral part of my life, I did not openly discuss because I learned at an early age that people are often afraid of what they do not understand. I had a wonderful childhood, but a challenging adult life: Two marriages; two divorces; being a single mom of four children for almost ten years before marrying my husband, Tom, in 2003. At that same time, I was also slowly opening up about my intuitive gifts, primarily due to the recent loss of my mother to breast cancer.

In late Spring of 2004, I made the personal commitment to embrace my intuitive abilities. I was ready to walk through any open door that God presented to me. That very evening, an email led me to connect with Deborah "Joy" Edgerton, a spiritual conference producer in Florida. Joy mentioned she had just had a speaker drop out of her Atlanta conference and asked if I would step in. Without a moment's hesitation, I said "yes!"

Joy and I became close "phone friends." Shortly thereafter, she moved back to Burlington, Vermont, where she had been raised. I visited Joy for a weekend that summer, my first time ever in Vermont, but the moment I crossed the state line I felt connected in a way I had never experienced; I felt I was home.

On Saturday morning, Joy said, "Oh, I forgot to mention that today is my parents' fiftieth wedding anniversary and we're having a cookout at my brother Jim's house tonight." Later, while on the way to Jim's, Joy casually remarked, "Did I ever tell you the sorta cool thing about my dad? He grew up on a dairy farm next door to Norman Rockwell in West Arlington, Vermont, and was best friends with the Rockwell sons. He also was Norman's most used Boy Scout model. He knows all the stories about the illustrations Norman painted while he lived in Vermont, and his parents were really close friends with Norman and Mary."

The hair was up on the back of my neck and I could feel my mother's presence strongly around me, a familiar sign that something major in my life was coming. I immediately blurted out, "He's got to write his memoirs!" to which Joy replied, "He won't do it. He's been interviewed and approached to write his book for more than thirty years, but he's just such a private man…but, maybe he'd let you do it!"

We arrived at Jim's house ahead of Bud and his wife Dot. When Jim heard I was a published author, he got excited about the possibility of my writing their father's story and we all hatched a plan to subtlely approach Bud during the evening. The doorbell rang and when Jim answered, from down the hall Joy and I heard him say:

"Hey Mom! Hey Dad! Happy Anniversary! Listen, Joy's friend Nan is a writer and she wants to write your book – TAKE IT, NAN!"

Bud quietly walked into the kitchen. I remember being struck by how handsome he was and thinking I could easily understand why Rockwell would have chosen him to model. As Bud looked at me without saying a word, I stammered to explain why I was the perfect person to write his memoirs. I don't exactly remember what I said, but when I was done he studied me for a full ten seconds and then said, "Ok. So, what do we do?" My mind racing, I committed on the spot to move to Vermont in a few weeks to start the interview-intensive work, to which Bud replied, "Ok, sounds good. Come 'round the house tomorrow and we'll put you on the family calendar." I knew I was in like flint then – in our house growing up, being on the family calendar was a solid commitment.

Six weeks later, my husband, two daughters (my sons were already grown), and I moved to Vermont. I began working on Bud's book, hungrily digesting his amazing near-encyclopedic recollection and recitation of facts and details that extensive research subsequently proved historically accurate. I delighted in meeting and interviewing all of the Rockwell sons, as well as the Edgerton sisters and cousins. Bud's and my numerous trips to Arlington, along with his easy storytelling style, intrigued this city girl who knew nothing of farming, hunting, or living in rural America. As a writer, I embraced the challenge of capturing Bud's cadence and speech so that the reader could enjoy in words what he and I had shared in conversation. The writing of the book truly took on a life of its own - so much more than a project! It was a journey of discovery that led to an insight and understanding of our country's history, our core values, and of an artist I had loved since childhood, Norman Rockwell.

While immersed in writing Bud's memoirs, I simultaneously expanded my intuitive work openly and publicly. In October 2006, I appeared on The Lana And Nolan In The Morning Show on

Burlington's WEZF, taking phone calls on air. A short time after, I was pleased with the opportunity to sign with international consulting agency, McVay Media. From 2007 to the present, I have enjoyed appearing regularly on morning shows throughout the U.S. In 2009, "The Nan O'Brien Show," a nationally-syndicated radio show, launched, as did my nationally-syndicated daily column, "Intuitively Yours by Nan O'Brien." Speaking engagements the last three years have taken me throughout the country and Canada as well, where I have had the privilege to meet and share with so many wonderful people. It has been quite a journey of discovery, too! Embracing opportunities; being true to self; living in gratitude; finding home.

Looking back at the events of the last five years, I can only smile in wonder at the evidence of God's plan for my life: The commitment to acknowledge my intuitive gifts publicly led me to Joy; who led me to her father, Bud; which presented me with an opportunity to use my writing abilities on an amazing project; which brought me to Vermont; which launched my intuitive career and a writing career opportunity of a lifetime; and which also allowed me the honor of becoming "family by heart" to Bud and Dot Edgerton, two of the dearest people I have ever known.

And while I never had the pleasure of meeting Jim, Clara, Norman, or Mary; and Bud never met my mother, I'd like to think that they are all smiling at us as I write this, as the second portrait of two American families has evolved from the first.

-Nan O'Brien